THE MOBS AND THE MAFIA

THE ILLUSTRATED HISTORY
OF ORGANIZED CRIME

THE MOBS AND THE MAFIA

by HANK MESSICK
and BURT GOLDBLATT

GALAHAD BOOKS · NEW YORK

To Mildred
H. M.

Library of Congress Catalog Card Number: 73-92830
ISBN 0-88365-211-0

Published by arrangement with T. Y. Crowell Company

Designed by Burt Goldblatt

Manufactured in the United States of America

Books by Hank Messick

THE SILENT SYNDICATE
SYNDICATE IN THE SUN
SYNDICATE WIFE
SYNDICATE ABROAD
SECRET FILE
LANSKY
JOHN EDGAR HOOVER

Books by Burt Goldblatt

HOW MANY ER'S ARE YOU
PORTRAIT OF CARNEGIE HALL
THE COUNTRY MUSIC STORY
THE MARX BROTHERS AT THE MOVIES
CINEMA OF THE FANTASTIC
THE WORLD SERIES

CONTENTS

*Crime is a kind of human behavior,
controlling it means changing the
hearts and minds of men.
President's Commission
on Law Enforcement, 1967*

INTRODUCTION

It is a sad commentary on disorganized society that no generally accepted definition of organized crime exists. The failure to define the problem has permitted myths and legends to abound and millions of words of near-nonsense to be written. There is no real mystery, however. When the nature of organized crime is understood the reasons why no definition has been achieved become very apparent.

In a study necessarily limited by space, it is even more essential that a definition be provided. For the purposes of this history one prepared for the New York Joint Legislative Committee on Crime will be used:

"Organized crime is a continuing conspiracy to gain money and power without regard for law by utilizing economic and physical force, public and private corruption, in an extension of the free-enterprise system."

When all romantic trappings are removed, gangsters emerge with the same objectives as legitimate businessmen. They are but more free with their enterprise. Nor are gangsters confined to one ethnic or national group. As to the rank and file gangsters en masse, the theory of ethnic succession is valid, but from a leadership point of view, men of all backgrounds are, and have been, active in key roles.

In many respects, organized crime is a product of historical accident. While men have always turned to crime as a shortcut to wealth, it was a combination of coincidences that made possible a national crime syndicate: the presence in this country of millions of hungry first-generation Americans; the easy profits of Prohibition; the Great Depression which left bootleggers with cash when banks lacked credit; the destruction of many big-city political machines under the New Deal; an alliance on the right of crime and politics; and the general loss by millions of traditional moral and social perspectives.

This short history offers an opportunity to put organized crime into focus. In the space available it cannot describe syndicate organization in every city, the thousands of gangland murders, the hundreds of political scandals. Nor can one cater to the "Godfather" image of the Mafia if perspective is to be achieved. But perhaps these limitations permit us for the first time to see the forest instead of the trees.

Much confusion in recent years has resulted from an overemphasis on the Mafia by some official agencies. Yet any serious student of that vendetta-ridden secret society will recognize the impossibility of the Mafia playing the role assigned to it. Despite many and varied formal charts of Mafia "families"—charts that were inaccurate to begin with and out of date before the ink had dried—the real structure of the Mafia has resembled a plate of spaghetti. The various strands are mixed up with each other, but it is impossible to make sense of the arrangement. In reality the Mafia is a state of mind, a blend of pride, greed, and ignorance. It is vanishing because the sociological conditions that made it possible have changed.

Throughout the history of organized crime there have been internal conflicts between men of passion and men of intellect. Most Mafia leaders belong in the first group, but not all men of Italian descent. John Torrio and Charles "Lucky" Luciano had brains as well as balls—to use a term employed by Meyer Lansky—and they looked upon the heroics of their colleagues with disgust. While the public concentrated on the Capones and the Bugsy Siegels, the quiet businessmen of crime worked with politicians and industry executives to make crime an integral part of our socioeconomic system. Organized crime has become not a wart on the fair face of Miss Liberty but a cancer of the blood. When this is understood, the promises of politicians to eliminate gangsters and restore law and order ring hollow indeed. Actually, the public has never really wanted to abolish crime or know too much about it. It is more fun to observe the tip of the iceberg and speculate as to what is really going on beneath the surface.

PROLOGUE—1972

In the nightclubs, the penthouses, the luxury condominiums of Miami Beach the arrival of 1972 was greeted with cheers, champagne, and kisses, but for the silent men watching the modest house in the "Little Havana" section of Miami it was just another night.

The vigil continued for four more days, the tension increasing with each passing hour.

On the evening of January 4, sudden activity inside the house alerted the watchers. Three men arrived, slipping in one by one at staggered intervals. Behind the curtains, lights burned and figures moved.

A taxi, obviously answering a call, pulled up on the dark street in front of the house at 3520 SW Fourth and honked. Instantly the three men emerged. Each was carrying a large suitcase. They got into the cab with their suitcases and moved away. Cars followed at a discreet distance. Quickly it became apparent that the taxi was headed toward Miami's sprawling international airport. A message flashed across the city. At the airport a reception committee formed.

Taking the upper ramp for departing passengers, the taxi stopped in front of the Eastern Airlines section of the terminal building. The men paid their driver and got out, ignoring a porter's offer to assist them with their luggage. Before they could enter the air-conditioned building, however, special agents of the Bureau of Narcotics and Dangerous Drugs surrounded them with drawn guns.

The men seemed stunned. They made no attempt to resist, to escape. A search revealed they were unarmed. It also disclosed they held tickets on the midnight flight to New York City.

The suitcases were opened. Inside were plastic bags containing 130 pounds of uncut heroin.

On the basis of the discovery, a search warrant was obtained within minutes and the house on Fourth Street was raided. One man and two young women were arrested. The special agents found another supply of pure heroin—108 pounds of it already packed in seven suitcases.

The roundup continued. Two days later, after the arrest of two more men who had frequently visited the little house during the

1

two weeks it had been under surveillance, the agents seized another 147 pounds of heroin. The total was now 385 pounds. Its value "on the street"—after being diluted to increase quantity—was officially estimated as $77 million.

In weight and in retail value the heroin seized was a record haul—the largest in history. Yet the special agents who made the coup were not satisfied. Even though the heroin had not reached the market, no serious harm had been done to the drug traffic. Bernard A. Theisen, the special agent-in-charge, noted that none of those arrested "could be considered important." They were "mules," nothing more, and as such they were easily expendable.

The new term, "mules," is an indication in itself of the revolution which in the past decade has taken place in the ancient narcotics racket. The old term was "courier," but it went out of fashion when control of the business passed from the hands of the Mafia. Of the eight persons arrrested, all had "Latin" names. Students of the Mafia of tradition would find no trace of an Italian-Sicilian secret society in this caper. For history had repeated itself and a new ethnic group had elbowed the old one aside.

As early as 1969, officials of the Bureau of Narcotics and Dangerous Drugs had dubbed the new group "the Cuban Mafia" in testimony before a Congressional subcommittee. Spokesmen for the Bureau

Peter Rankin, left, of
the Bureau of
Narcotics and
Dangerous Drugs,
displays 147 pounds
of heroin taken in a
raid in Miami in 1972.
Above, five of the
eight people arrested
in what was the
largest heroin seizure
in history.

James R. Hoffa, center of picture, former president of the International Brotherhood of Teamsters, convicted of tampering with a federal jury in 1964, watches a baseball game at Lewisburg Federal Penitentiary.

4

emphasized, however, that the name was for convenience only. There was no relationship, they said, to "the Italian Mafia."

Members of "the Cuban Mafia" learned the business of crime in the days when Cuban President Fulgencio Batista cooperated with crime syndicate boss Meyer Lansky in operating a huge gambling empire in Havana. When Fidel Castro sent Batista and Lansky fleeing in 1959, the hungry Cubans were forced to seek new shortcuts to easy money. They found it on the slopes of the Andes Mountains in South America where the coca leaf grows wild and provides raw material for the deadly drug cocaine. Quickly, an international traffic in cocaine was organized. So successful were the Cubans and their eager allies in setting up "mule trains" to the United States that they branched out into that more popular staple —heroin.

The Mafia, disorganized, fragmented, and the target of every ambitious politician, made no effort to defend what had been its exclusive franchise for years. A new era in the history of organized crime had begun. Decades might pass before the new leaders would be identified.

Thus the capture of $77 million worth of heroin in the first week of 1972 served largely to illustrate how the drug traffic had grown. The increasing use of narcotics throughout the country made it plain that for every pound seized in transit, hundreds of other pounds got through to the retailers. A demand had been created and, as the Prohibition decade proved, men would supply that demand if the rewards were large enough. For one thing does not change—the desire for fast bucks.

There were ironic reminders, as the new year dawned on a deepening drug crisis, of past battles in society's struggle to protect itself from itself.

Item: Thomas "Yonnie" Licavoli, once a hired gun for the Purple Gang of Detroit, was finally paroled from prison after serving thirty-six years for murder.

Item: Mickey Cohen, successor to the slain Bugsy Siegel as syndicate boss of the West, was released from prison after serving ten years for income-tax evasion. Some editorial writers, noting that Cohen suffered brain damage in prison when beaten by a fellow prisoner, cited his condition as proof crime doesn't pay.

Item: James R. Hoffa, former boss of the Teamsters Union, went free when President Nixon personally intervened on his behalf. As the man who controlled millions in union pension funds, Hoffa was once a most important figure in organized crime. Robert F. Kennedy had pursued him with a zeal unique in law-enforcement circles, so that Hoffa was able to convince many of the cynical that he was the victim of a personal vendetta. But in 1972, Kennedy was dead; his political foes were in power and facing a new election. Hoffa was still a man of influence and could help. Besides, it was the Christmas season and, yes, Jimmy, there is a Santa Claus.

Item: J. Edgar Hoover celebrated his seventy-sixth birthday on January 1, 1972, and announced he had no plans to quit as director of the Federal Bureau of Investigation.

In the forty-eight years Hoover had been FBI boss and the country's leading lawman, ethnic gangs had united in local "combinations." Regional syndicates had developed and a loose alliance on the national level became a reality. The Syndicate International had followed. In short, organized crime had become an integrated part of the socio-economic life of the nation.

A new year . . . a new chapter . . . a new knock on the door. So it has been, so it will be, as the history of organized crime remains a volume without an ending.

But there is a beginning. . . .

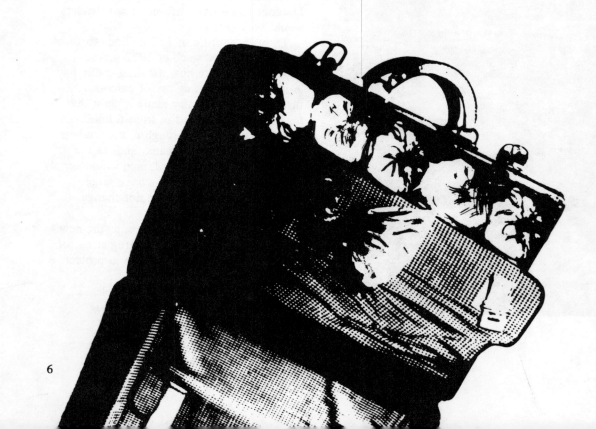

I THE PROMISED LAND

In 1903, Nicola Gentile, a native of Siculiana, Sicily, finding no opportunity to learn a trade in his native village, stowed away on a ship and came to America as a youth. Although barely able to read or write, he, in his own words, possessed "an uncommon strength of will to be sinister," a trait that was soon to bring him high rank in the Mafia.

"I looked very much like many of the poor Italian immigrants disembarking at the Port of New York with their only bag on their shoulders and with red polka-dot handkerchiefs fastened above their eyes," said Gentile years later. "I, even so, instead, reached land with a tattered suitcase tied with a piece of cord. A sailor brought me to the house of my countryman, Domenico Taormina, at 91 Elizabeth Street, who, after this, gave me a ticket for Kansas City where I arrived with a trainload of immigrants after a trip of better than six days."

Nicola was seeking an older brother who had come earlier to the States and who, along with thousands of other immigrants, was working on a railroad in Kansas. The boy was awed by the "immeasurable rows of buildings, the endless streets," but it was the attitude of the people that most impressed him. They walked briskly, giving him the impression that all "had an urgent mission to perform."

"What a contrast with the inhabitants of my town," he commented. "People who, when they walked, studied their manner of walking so that their slow strut made them appear solemn, with the thumb of the right hand hooked in the belt of the pants, with the cap tilted over the right eye, trying to create an arrogant air that should command respect."

This sketch of attitudes tells much about why such a secret society as the Mafia should flourish in Sicily and could be transplanted to the ghettos of the New World. But implicit here is also the reason why, inevitably, it would die when the new arrivals began to walk as briskly as those who put down roots much earlier. Consider Gentile's account of the organization, the "Honored Society," as he liked to call it in his old age:

"The organization originated many, many

years ago in antiquity and it gives the right to defend the honor, the weak, and to respect the human law. If today the daily papers in their articles, and public opinion, point to it as a running sore on our country, they can't be blamed because they [the Mafia members] have now degenerated and with scoundrelism have put their hands into the wellsprings of production and have formed somewhat monopolies.

"All organizations are born with principles and humanitarian goals, but in their midst the opportunists are never missing and will try to make a profit. With this I don't want to apologize for the Honored Society, or Mafia, as it is commonly called; it would be just as if I would admit a state within a state. The Honored Society I could compare, for its assistance to the associates, to the Masons. But the Masons' teachings are mystical or theological. The Honored Society finds its reasons for existence in force and in terror. However, it was started by landowners as a disciplinary force in the community. It was started in the least developed part of Sicily, and was brought to America in the sections of the country where Sicilians, Calabrians, and Neapolitans lived.

"Their associates are called *fratellos* and they obey a *capo* elected by them. The capo afterwards picks the *consigliari* [counsellors] that help him to work out justice and make judgments. When one of them [the fratellos] finds himself in difficulty of any kind, the association tries to help and assist him.

"With the passing of time in every city of America these associations were formed. In the city of New York and Brooklyn alone there were five. Between the heads of the various *borgates* or families, they select the overall capo whom they call the capo di capi re, or king. That means the re of the Honored Society. At New York and Brooklyn among the five borgates there are 2,000 associates.

"My temperament," concluded Gentile,

9

"Send these, the homeless, tempest-tost to me . . ."

91 Elizabeth Street in New York looks much the same today as it must have when Nicola Gentile, just off the boat from Sicily, stayed there in 1903. Gentile later became a leader of several Mafia families. In 1937, his fortunes declined drastically. He is shown after his arrest in New Orleans on a narcotics charge. In 1972, a few short blocks from Elizabeth Street, Joseph "Crazy Joe" Gallo, who led a rebellion against his Mafia family, was gunned down while celebrating his 43rd birthday.

10

"was bringing me a life of adventure. The courage which nature had endowed me, my intrepid spirit and imperious nature, and my code which I thought was right, made me join the Honored Society."

In those first years the Mafia in America was much like the Mafia in Sicily; it preyed on nonmembers among its own countrymen. Immigrants unaccustomed to the laws, traditions, and language of the United States were easy victims of extortion and could be forced to contribute a percentage of their small earnings as they had done in the old country. The "signature" of the Mafia was a black handprint, and for some years the secret society was known as the Black Hand. Members of the organization were, of course, exempt from the list of potential victims, and this acted as an inducement to recruitment.

Gentile told of settling a feud between uncle and nephew by the simple expedient of making the nephew a member of the Honored Society too. The uncle, who had been threatening to kill his brother's son, quickly forgot his anger "and the two started to love one another." Gentile had created a relationship stronger than blood alone.

It was by such acts of kindness that Gentile, if his account is to be believed, gradually worked himself up to the role of Mafia troubleshooter in the United States. Since betrayals and vendettas were second nature to Mafia members, a peacemaker was badly needed. Over a period of years, "Uncle Cola," as he became known, ranged from New York to San Francisco settling internal problems, and actually serving as capo in several cities.

The Italian-Sicilian was not the only newcomer to the Promised Land of America. Earlier the Germans and Irish and then the Eastern European Jew had come in great waves—fleeing from hunger and religious persecution. Not only did these new arrivals find competition and even conflict with other

GIVES TO BLACK HAND

Tenor Caruso Pays $2,000 in Response to Threats.

GREATER SUM IS DEMAN...

Famous Singer Is Willing ... munity, but the Police ... Him Closely in Hope ... tortionists—Two Pr... Indicted—Many Pa...

New York, Mar... the indictment ... ous Italian bur... cotte and Misiano, ... on March 4, charge...

SCARE FOR CARUSO

TRICK LEADS TO TWO ARRESTS.

Tenor Alarmed by Letters Demanding $15,000—Police Decoy Baits Trap.

Antonio Cinbotta, a saloon keeper, of No. 188 Columbia street, Brooklyn ... Anton... ...th at...

TERRIBLE GUN FOR CARUSO

IF IT WAS THE ONE FOUND ON THE SICILIAN MISIANI.

$1,500 Bail Police Records tures—Brook. olice at Odds.

go to Police to have a look are suspected g letters. There lice thought, of lly known to the deemed wise to vous strain under since he got the Caruso's pres. sary in the Adams e court. where the gred. since they

The Black Hand, which operated mainly in the United States, specialized in the intimidation and extortion of Italian immigrants. One of their victims was Enrico Caruso, the leading tenor of the Metropolitan Opera.

12

Caruso received three Black Hand letters similar to the one at right. He paid $2,000, but when $15,000 was demanded he went to the police. His orders were to leave the money under a stoop of a factory building. The police set a trap and caught two Italian businessmen.

ethnic groups, but perhaps their most difficult adjustment was in accepting the firmly established "unofficial religion" of American society—the Puritan Ethic.

The ideals upon which the Puritan Ethic was based reflected the WASP—white Anglo-Saxon Protestant—background of those earlier immigrants who took the land away from the Indians. The Puritan Ethic was predicated on the belief that God would reward on earth, as well as in a future heaven, those who obeyed His laws, worked hard, and lived as an example to others. Thus the accumulation of wealth was seen as proof of God's favor and evidence of a moral life.

That this was a convenient faith, tailored to the needs of a pioneer society, there can be no doubt. That there was also much hypocrisy in the practice of such a faith is also without question. But no student of history can doubt that the vast majority of citizens, generation after generation, took it all most seriously and ascribed the development and prosperity of the United States to the principles of the Puritan Ethic.

It was into this settled, ordered, and complacent world that representatives of different faiths were thrust in great numbers in the two decades before the Great War. The new arrivals poured into East Coast cities, pausing in ghettos not unlike the ones they left behind, and going on to inland cities as employment opportunities developed. With jobs the motivating force, strange patterns evolved. Italians built railroads in New England, then settled down to run grocery stores. The shrimp industry offered experienced hands opportunity along the Gulf Coast of Mississippi, and an Italian colony was planted in Biloxi. The sponge industry brought many Greeks to Tarpon Springs on the west coast of Florida. The steel mills of the Ohio valley needed strong backs, and many southern Europeans found jobs and homes in Youngstown, Pittsburgh,

and Gary. Boston, where the Puritan Ethic had its home, was divided into ethnic districts. The Old North Church, known to every school child since the Revolution, became hemmed in and squeezed by an Italian colony until one could almost believe the building had been moved physically to Rome.

What happened when these newcomers came face to face with the Puritan Ethic? As Will Herberg put it: "The newcomer is expected to change many things about him as he becomes American—nationality, language, culture. One thing, however, he is not expected to change, and that is his religion." Yet under the Puritan Ethic, religion was bound up with the economy in that God was supposed to reward moral man with material wealth. To the newcomer, America was indeed the Promised Land, a place where even an immigrant could get rich quick. In short, he approved of the rewards of the Puritan Ethic without understanding—or at least accepting—the ideals of moral conduct that were supposed to earn the reward.

The first arrivals were not aware of the problem. Frightened by the new freedom, most of them were content with the New World ghettos where language and custom were familiar. It remained for their sons, some brought to this country as children and others native-born Americans, to sense the basic conflict. Excited by the wealth of the New World and the social freedom it offered, the children became impatient with their elders and the old way of life they represented. If to achieve personal position quickly it was necessary to ignore the moral aspects of the Puritan Ethic, so be it. Drawing upon their more liberal religion—or simply ignoring all questions of morality—they claimed the right to disregard man-made laws that interfered with their pursuit of the fast buck.

As they saw it, the WASPs had just arrived early, established themselves, and

15

The Chinese tongs, organized in the United States in the Western goldfields about 1860, became mainly associations controlling gambling and opium-smoking privileges. During the height of their power, almost every store in New York's Chinatown had games of chance; and the fumes of opium from rooms above or basements below floated down the street. In the great tong war of 1909, over 50 were killed and several times that number wounded, and there was much property destruction by bombs, as the Chinese had begun to experiment with dynamite.

Police Keep Close Watch
After Sunday's Tong Fight.

ARRAIGN SEVEN CELESTIALS

THREE MORE SHOT
IN A TONG BATTLE

Chinatown

POLICE GUARD
CHINESE SHOPS TO
AVERT TONG WAR

BY WILL

ONE DEAD, ONE DYING
IN CHINESE SHOOTING

The Four Brothers Celebration
Starts with Battle in Streets
of Chinatown.

DIDN'T STOP FEAST, THOUGH

After Smoke of Conflict Clears
Members Were Anxious
About Feed—Police
Make Arrests.

then set up a lot of hypocritical laws to protect their personal empires. Under what Gentile called "the human law," they also had the right to take what they could get. This, in effect, was the law of the jungle, and it gives justification to organized crime today. Others turned to more sophisticated arguments, claiming, in effect, that once they made a lot of money they could "earn" God's blessing by doing good deeds with a portion of their wealth. Many universities have profited from this line of thought in the subsequent decades.

Not too many shortcuts to wealth—great wealth—existed in the first twenty years of the century, but organized crime began taking shape nonetheless. The sale of female flesh offered one opportunity for organizational ability, and newspaper-circulation wars served as training schools for future crime syndicate enforcers. The one complemented the other, since sensational stories about white slavers earned newspapers many new readers, and who controlled which street corner became important to circulation managers.

The so-called "white slave trade" was in itself an outgrowth of the continuing population explosion fueled by immigration. Many of the customers were hard-working immigrants who had left their wives in the old country while they labored to earn their passage. Such men needed a woman occasionally and, logically enough, they wanted one who resembled their wives or at least spoke the same language. Many of these girls were the daughters of immigrants who, unable to find husbands, turned to prostitution as a shortcut to a better life. Others were tricked by "ropers" who seduced them or promised to find them good-paying jobs in distant cities. In some cities such as Chicago, regular "barracks" were maintained for training or "breaking" new girls. Specialists would rape an unwilling girl repeatedly until her spirit was at last

GIRL SLAVES TELL TALES OF HORROR.

Two More Taken from Bondage in Raids Directed by U. S. District Attorney

CRUSADE AGAINST "DEBT"

Judge Crowe Starts Campaign to Wipe Out Means for Holding Women in Resorts.

Inhumanities practiced on white slaves were revealed yesterday in the confes...

USE NEW WHITE SLAVE LAW

Police Arrest Two Men C... with Illegal Trafficking

FINES EMPLOYMENT AGEN...

...dge Newcomer Finds Margaret Hoen and H. G. Enright Guilty.

...arrests were made yesterday under ...state law which provides the penal-... trafficking in " white slaves." ... Alperan, 248 Washington boule-...d Louis Harris, 356 West Madison ...der the new statute may be pun-...imprisonment in the penitentiary ...to which may be added a fine ...were ...

INDICTS 60 "WHITE SLAVERS"

Federal Grand Jury Returns Bills Against Keepers of Resorts.

PLANS FOR MORE RAIDS.

District Attorney Sims Will Continue Raids in the Levees.

The federal grand jury adjourned yester-day until Monday morning after returning fifty indictments against " white slave " keepers. District Attorney Sims and his as-sociates, however, continued their crusade. The objects of the latest raids are the re-sorts of South Chicago. A raid was mad... Thursday ... and three ...

VICE

Fifty ... Again...

FOUR ...

...strict Att... Tr...

...n a ro... e new ... ecome ...ned ... ...ters ... ...y...

shattered. Those girls of better than average looks and fatalism were given special training and graduated to brothels catering to higher-income customers. At intervals "auctions" would be held at the various barracks and scores of girls would be sold to the highest bidders.

To find and entrap sufficient numbers of young women to meet the demand required rather large organizations, sometimes reaching from midwestern cities halfway across the continent to ports on both coasts. The transportation and training of the new slaves also involved considerable capital and personnel. Thus the groundwork for future syndicates was prepared. The growing problem was recognized in 1910 when the White Slave Traffic Act was passed by Congress. It prohibited the transportation of females in interstate commerce. Better known as the Mann Act, the law is still on the books today but serves primarily to embarrass businessmen who may stray across a state line in search of a motel. Enforcement of the new law was assigned to the two-year-old Bureau of Investigation (later the FBI), and set a precedent permitting the Bureau's powers in future years to be expanded whenever interstate commerce was involved.

Perhaps the most famous white slaver—famous because he prepared the way for John "the Fox" Torrio and Al Capone—was James "Big Jim" Colosimo. Born in 1871 in Italy, Colosimo got a jump on many of his countrymen by coming to the United States in 1881. His father brought him to the red-light district of Chicago known as the Levee, and in 1902, having achieved some political influence, Big Jim married a leading madam. Soon he was managing a string of brothels and, inevitably, organized a white-slave gang to keep his brothels supplied with fresh bodies. Torrio, a nephew, was brought from New York to serve as executive assistant and gradually took over Colosimo's business and built it up into an empire.

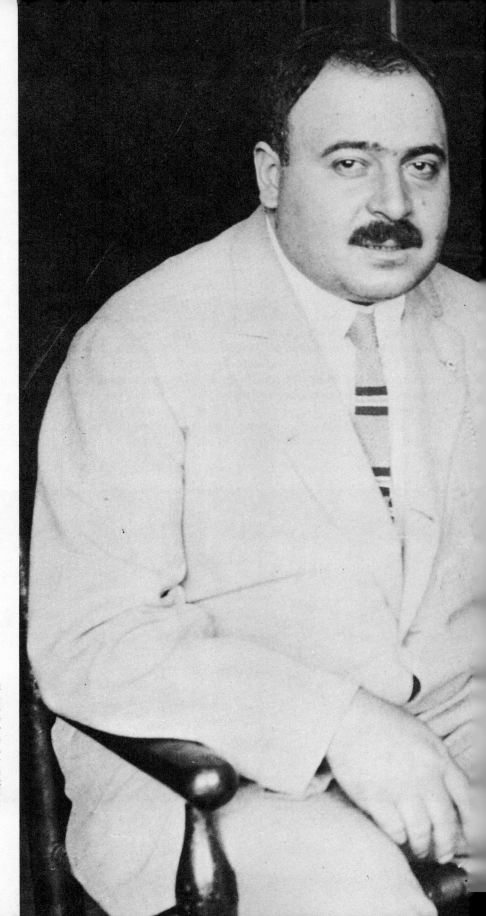

Big Jim Colosimo, at left, shown here with his lawyer, Charles Erbstein, ruled the underworld longer than any other one man in Chicago's history. The law rarely bothered him but he was constant prey to Black Hand extortionists.

20

Colosimo, center, is shown with his first wife, left, a former brothel owner; her sister; his father, and young John Torrio. Opposite page, Big Jim with his girl friend, Dale Winter, a musical-comedy actress who sang in his cafe. Less than three weeks after they were married, he was slain.

Torrio, with Arnold Rothstein and Meyer Lansky, were the principal architects of the national crime syndicate as it evolved and developed over the next half-century. The genius of such men has been largely the ability to recognize when, due to economic or sociological reasons, one racket is ready to be supplanted by another. Thus Torrio was able to discern that while vice—the sale of sex—would always remain profitable, the peculiar circumstances that had made white slavery *logical* were vanishing. Ahead loomed new opportunity in the illicit liquor business. When Colosimo was unable or at least unwilling to change with the times, Torrio simply had him murdered on May 11, 1920, and took over as boss. In a real way he symbolized the revolt of the second-generation Americans against the Old World attitudes of their elders, the so-called "Mustache Petes."

With millions of new voters pouring into the country and a natural exodus to the city from the farm underway, politicians found themselves devising new methods of influencing the electorate. The press assumed new importance, but to be useful newspapers had to be cheap and interesting. Soon great circulation wars developed, inspired less by the publishers than by the politician supported by the publishers. Even today newspaper editors cling to the notion that they are potential kingmakers and the impulse to "play politics" is sometimes irresistible. Then as now, however, a newspaper's real influence is in the manner it presents the news, not in the thunderbolts flashing on the editorial pages.

Horatio Alger could, and did, write inspiring books such as *Rough and Ready* about newsboys who defended their street corner and their right to sell newspapers for two cents each, but the competition in reality was something less than heroic.

Arthur B. "Mickey" McBride was hired in 1913 to be circulator of the Cleveland

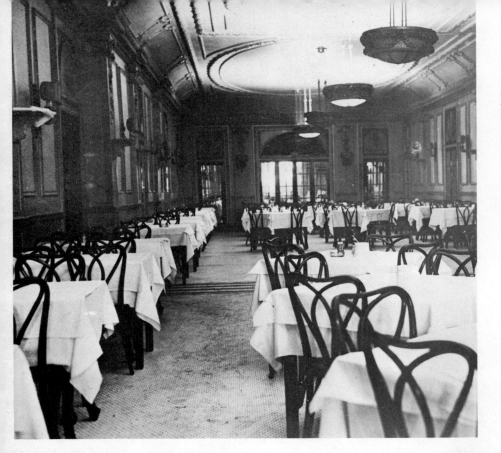

Colosimo's Restaurant was a center of Chicago's nightlife and a favorite spot for slumming parties. Opera stars John McCormack and Luisa Tetrazzini were among its patrons. At right, the crowd outside the restaurant the day Big Jim was shot in the lobby.

Chicago THE WORLD'S GREATEST NEWSPAPER Daily Tribune.

FINAL EDITION

VME LXXIX.—NO. 114. C.   COPYRIGHT 1920 BY THE TRIBUNE COMPANY.   WEDNESDAY, MAY 12, 1920—32 PAGES. THIS PAPER CONSISTS OF TWO SECTIONS—SECTION ONE   ** PRICE TWO CENTS IN CHICAGO

OLOSIMO SLAIN; SEEK EX-WIFE, JUST RETURNED

CE OPENS -QUARTER T ON REDS

Federation Is d Dissolved.

By Foreign News Service
Special Cable.
By the Tribune Company.)
— Paris tonight is re-
arance of May 1.

possible disorders as a
government's move to the
radical
controlled by the radical
nister of war has placed
of cavalry are coming
om the suburbs
loaded with gendarmes
rush at a moment's
scene of any trouble
re are under arms in

e decade if the situation
ghting the troops will
but the cavalry com-
ll disciplined and too
encourages the idea of

Cabinet Order
ne taken by the mi-
Howard state Duca of
abinet to Minister of
eau to open proceed

BANKERS HOPE TO CLAMP LID ON SPENDING ORGY.

Loan Only Essential Industry, Plan.

BY ARTHUR SEARS HENNING.

Washington, D. C., May 11.—[Spe-
cial.]—How to halt the orgy of spending on luxuries and other nonessentials
in which Americans are indulging and
divert capital to increasing production
of necessities which will reduce the
cost of living, is a question that will
be considered by leading bankers in a
conference with Secretary of the Treasury Houston and the federal reserve
board next week.

The principal suggestion to be discussed is that the reserve banks and
the bankers take concerted action to
curtail the advance of credit for the
production of nonessentials in an effort to stem the wave of extravagance
on the theory the people will stop
spending when there are no luxuries
to buy and capital will be forced into
the more profitable field of none
essentials.

Chicago Bankers to Attend.

George M. Reynolds and James B.
Forgan of Chicago will take a leading
part in the conference, the former as
a as A director of the Chicago federal reserve bank and the latter in his
his capacity of member of the ad-
visory council of the federal reserve
system and chairman of the American
Bankers association committee appointed for the conference

THE PROGRESSIVE WING OF THE REPUBLICAN PARTY IN ILLINOIS
(AS NICKNAMED BY MR. HEARST.)

[Copyright 1920 By The Chicago Tribune.]

FIGHT ALL DAY IN THE DEFENSE OF CARRANZA

U. S. Consul Reports Mexico Is Quiet.

BULLETIN

Vera Cruz, May 11—Forces commanded by President Carranza
fought an all day battle today
against rebel troops under Gen Hill
and Gen Trevine between San Mar-
cos, in the state of Puebla, and Hua-
mantla, in the state of Tlaxacala
according to advices received here

Brownsville, Tex. May 11: An
agreement may be reached whereas
the reconstituted w gain control
Matamoros the battery own c
vertter of Mexico order
incident Carranza and r g
late sources in Matamoros
tng It is said there is a gen a
fort of army officers in Matamoros
n o a conf service the fol a
reach that a revolt completo
arch ment of a torn to the Amer c
and of the unequivocal bridge a scene
two in the gone were by t a gover
ton pushing toward M
The bridge had bee
pairs but Unite

5 Face Noose as Brislane Is Doomed to Die

Dashing Eddie Brislane slayer of
William Mills, got his name on the
hangman's waiting list last night—the
fifth name entered on that roll in ten
days—and Robert Carter was sent
enced to life imprisonment.
The Criminal court, with its increased force of judges, is giving quick
justice to prisoners charged with murder. The dockets of the court soon will
be cleaned

Final Liquor Insanity

Brislane and Carter were found
guilty by a jury in Judge Kickham
an convert after it had deliberated
a The five men had gone in
the of the theater to rob the cash
drawer at encountering Mills
Brislane fired. The defendants pleaded they were intoxicated to the point
of insanity

Brislane's two sisters. Mrs Alberta
Weber and Miss Marjorie Brislane, became hysterical when they heard him
sentenced to the gallows.

Carter's Bride Faints.

After they had been carried from the
court room the clerk read the verdict
in the case of Carter. Mrs. Carter a
bride, he, and sister-in-law was carried
out in a faint

The other cases on the hangman's
waiting list are those of Frank Zagar, who
murdered his wife near Hubbard;
Flavio Lampino, Thomas Errico and
Nicholas Lana, charged with a number
of murders

Antil is likewise to be hanged June
for the murder of his wife

SHOT DOWN IN HIS OWN CAFE; SLAYER FLEES

Bride of 3 Weeks Mourns Loss.

"Big Jim" Colosimo was shot to
death in his cafe yesterday afternoon
by a person who came upon him alone,
sent a single bullet through his brain,
and then sped away unobserved

By his death Mrs. Dale Winter Colosimo his wife for only three weeks,
was widowed. Mrs Vittoria Moresco
Colosimo divorced only a month became the feature in a city wide search
by the police

Chicago's underworld was in turmoil.
The Colosimo murder, the Coleman murder, all the crimes that have emphasized Chicago's Camorra as a thing beyond Chicago's law, all came under police
scrutiny for clews in this latest and
boldest of assassinations

Slayer Only Witness.

Only the slayer saw Jim Colosimo
die. No word came from his lips after
he was found by his secretary and
friend. Frank Camilla. But on
their knowledge of Chicago gunmen,
of "Big Jim's" family life, of his business affairs and of the movements of
his friends and enemies, police last
were upon which

COLOSIMO'S RESTAURANT   2128   SERVICE TIRE AND REPAIR SHOP

Colosimo's funeral was the first of the gaudy displays in fashion in the 1920s in Chicago. Among the pallbearers were three judges, a congressman, and nine aldermen, walking side by side with white-slavers and gangsters. His widow, Dale Winter, above left, became a Broadway star within a month. Above, Moses Annenberg, founder of the number-one racing news wire service.

Arthur B. "Mickey" McBride at the
1951 Kefauver hearings.

His rival, Thomas J. McGinty, also
on hand to testify.

News. Allied with him was James Ragen, circulator of the Cleveland *Leader.* Both papers were owned by the family of the late political boss Mark Hanna. Opposed to McBride and Ragen was the circulation manager of the rival Cleveland *Plain Dealer,* Thomas J. McGinty.

McBride was born in Chicago in 1886, and won a reputation as a tough guy with organizational ability. He was to demonstrate that toughness again and again in years to come. After quitting the newspaper business he became king of the cabs in Cleveland, crushing his opposition as thoroughly as he had in the newspaper-circulation wars. In 1940, when Moses Annenberg, founder of the national wire service for bookies, went to prison, McBride and his old friend Ragen took charge and gave the wire service a new name—Continental Press. When Ragen was murdered, McBride became sole owner of the far-flung organization and ran it until the Kefauver Committee put it out of business in 1951. Meanwhile, McBride formed a professional football team, the Cleveland Browns, thus demonstrating once again his ability to organize violence and make it profitable. Eventually he sold the team to

Morris "Mushy" Wexler, Cleveland
wire service magnate, in 1951.

Alfred "Big Al" Polizzi is sworn in
at the Kefauver hearings.

Saul Silberman, owner of a syndicate-controlled horse track in Miami, and retired.

His rival McGinty was born in Cleveland in 1892, the youngest of eight children. His father, a dockworker, died when the boy was a baby and he was given to an older sister whose husband, a Cleveland fireman, became a father to him. McGinty worked first as a newspaper circulator and then turned boxer in an effort to make more profitable use of his fighting ability. One day, however, the light dawned. He was flat on his back, knocked there by "Battling Schultz," and over in his corner his manager was yelling for him to get up and take another punch. The young Irishman decided then and there to become a fight manager. It was easy enough to become a "sportsman" in those days, and, from that humble beginning McGinty went on to own race tracks, nightclubs, and gambling casinos from Cleveland to Miami, from Las Vegas to Havana. Ultimately he retired to a mansion near the ocean in Palm Beach, Florida.

In 1913, however, both men recruited armies of young punks, tough guys, who, armed with brass knuckles and lead pipes, fought each other for control of choice street corners in Cleveland. Such men as Alfred "Big Al" Polizzi, Fred Angersola, Morris "Mushy" Wexler, and many others got their start in the circulation wars and went on to become important figures in organized crime. And what was happening in Cleveland was happening in every other major city at the same time. Had someone set out deliberately to provide an army of strong-arm goons for use in Prohibition, it could not have been better planned.

Cleveland, of course, was just one of those cities that proved so attractive to immigrants. They settled initially in the Woodland district: the Irish first, and then, in the period we are most concerned with, the Jews and the Italians. In 1917 more than half of all children in school spoke a language other than English. By 1923, only 35.4 percent of public school children were of unmixed white

During the early 1900s immigration to the United States continued at a high rate; seven out of ten immigrants came from southern and eastern Europe. These newcomers, herded into the urban slums, contributed heavily to crime.

American parentage. Cleveland had the fourth largest Jewish population of any city in the United States.

As the immigrants adjusted to the new life and found a measure of prosperity they moved out to suburban areas—specific localities attracting specific ethnic groups— and left Woodland to the next wave of immigrants. After the Jews came the Italians. In 1920 the Italians numbered 14.9 percent in the Woodland district. By 1930, however, the Italians had begun their move to the suburbs, settling in the Mayfield Road area, to be replaced by the Negroes—moving up from the Deep South.

Some final figures help put the developing problem into perspective—for it was not to achieve full flower until Prohibition provided an easy source of wealth. Of 998 murders committed in Cleveland from 1918 to 1930, 213 occurred in the Woodland district. Of 373 brothels found in eight separate surveys, 98 were in the Woodland district.

Similar areas existed in every major city, attracting large numbers of immigrants, and similar population movements occurred in each. And it is no reflection on race or national origin to note that the ghetto areas have been breeding places for crime regardless of which group happened to be living there at the time. The temptation to take shortcuts to achieve the "American Way of Life" by ignoring the moral restrictions of the Puritan Ethic becomes stronger with each generation.

It is convenient to assume, as do many writers, that gangs began with Prohibition or—if you believe the FBI's version of events—with the economic depression of the 1930s. That both are mistaken assumptions only a superficial glance at history will make clear.

The pre-Prohibition gangs were closely related to the first organized activity of the bootlegging era largely because the early gangs were ethnic in nature. Street gangs

The ghettos in every major city where the new immigrants settled had much the same appearance as New York's Lower East Side.

usually are ethnic. They evolve to protect the pride, and the territory, of one ethnic group against another, and to give young toughs a "respectable" outlet for their frustrations and repressed ambitions.

Ironically, in view of the FBI's reputation, the gangs of the 1930s led by John Dillinger, Alvin Karpis, and the like, were more closely related to Jesse James than to the crime syndicates even then gaining power and influence. Out of the bitterness and poverty of the Reconstruction period following the Civil War came several groups of western outlaws who today are folk heroes. Out of the bitterness and poverty of the Great Depression came teams of bank robbers who already are almost folk heroes in the manner of Bonnie and Clyde. In both eras, the outlaws lived and died violently, depending on wits and their shooting irons, and having nothing in common with syndicate gangsters who made a million times more money in comparative safety by

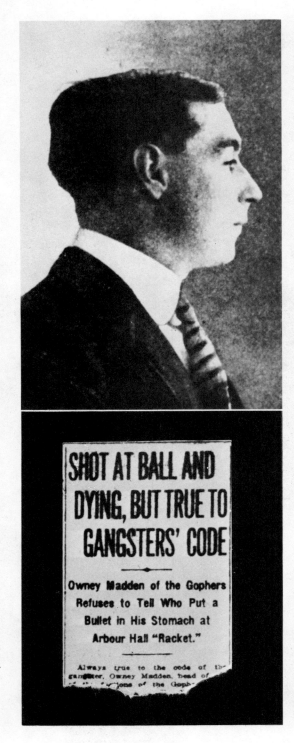

SHOT AT BALL AND DYING, BUT TRUE TO GANGSTERS' CODE

Owney Madden of the Gophers Refuses to Tell Who Put a Bullet in His Stomach at Arbour Hall "Racket."

Always true to the code of the gangster, Owney Madden, head of ... ... ions of the Goph-

Owney "the Killer" Madden started in stick-ups and extortion. He was bold, cunning, and cruel, and boasted he would be king of all the gangs. Many attempts were made to kill him. When he stopped six bullets in 1912, at the hands of 11 gunmen, the papers reported he was dying.

catering to the desires of the public.

Every large city had its gangs in the two decades before Prohibition. The Gophers in New York were perhaps more advanced than some since they included youths of several ethnic groups—a forerunner of the "combinations" of the third stage of Prohibition. The reason was the leader who emerged about 1910—Owney "the Killer" Madden.

Born in England—another unique feature, Madden was eleven when brought to this country. When he took command of the Gophers at eighteen, Owney was already famous as "the Killer." Slim, handsome, arrogant, he was a crack shot with revolver and slingshot, and an expert in the use of a lead pipe wrapped in newspaper. Repeatedly he was accused of murder. In every case the witnesses vanished, and Owney's reputation grew.

On November 6, 1912, a dance was under way at Fifty-second Street near

Madden recovered and did a term in jail for complicity in a gang killing. Released in 1923, he rapidly made a name as a bootlegger, hijacker, and gunman. By the 1940s, slim, dapper Madden had made too many enemies. The Syndicate permitted him to retire to Hot Springs, Ark.

Seventh Avenue. In walked Madden. Instantly the music stopped. Smiling, Owney waited a long moment and then graciously waved his hand to the scared musicians:

"Go on and have your fun," he said. "I won't bump off anybody here tonight."

Hastily, the musicians began to play; the dance resumed. Madden sat down at a table on a balcony overlooking the dance floor. A girl appeared, engaged his interest, caused him to relax his guard. Eleven men sidled onto the balcony and arranged themselves behind him before he noticed them. Standing up to face them, he issued an invitation:

"Come on, youse guys. Who did youse ever bump off?"

Guns blazed, and Madden went down with six bullets in him. True to underworld tradition, he refused to talk to police. "It's nobody's business but mine who put these slugs in me," he told them. In less than a week, as Owney recovered in the hospital, the three leaders of the gang that had shot him were murdered.

Eventually, after Owney had eliminated a challenge to his leadership, a girl friend sought revenge and talked. Madden was sentenced to Sing Sing for ten to twenty years. He was paroled in 1923, just in time to get in on the ground floor of the still developing booze business. From teen-age gangs to liquor syndicates was an easy step for Owney. Later he was to make a similar transition from booze to gambling. In the history of organized crime, "the Killer" was to be a major and, in time, an honored figure.

Towering above Madden and everyone else was, of course, Arnold "the Brain" Rothstein, "the man who dwells in doorways," the "King of Gamblers."

Rothstein was born in 1882 in New York, the second son of Abraham and Esther Rothstein whose parents had come from Bessarabia years before. The father was a good man who achieved a modest success in the dry goods business by hard work and good will. The failure of Arnold to follow in the paths of righteousness sincerely troubled the old man, who had been taught "to honor all men and love them as brothers." Perhaps it was Arnold's inability to love his older brother, Harry, that was at the root of the problem. At age three, Arnold tried to kill Harry with a knife, and the rivalry grew with the years. When Harry proved a brilliant student with ambitions to become a rabbi, Arnold tried to abandon both his studies and his religion. His father taught him about Jewish history, but, almost as if speaking for thousands of other "young Americans," Arnold replied:

"Who cares about that stuff? This is America, not Jerusalem. I'm an American. Let Harry be a Jew."

At age sixteen he dropped out of high school and set out to educate himself on the streets. Gambling appealed to him, and he had a knack for numbers. He quickly learned the art of playing the percentages and he was wise enough to invest some of his winnings in drinks for older, tougher boys. In a sense he was buying protection, a commodity he would have much need of in his short career. As soon as he had a "roll" put together, he began hanging around the crap games so prevalent in the area and making loans to the players as the need arose. The borrower had one week to return five dollars for every four provided by Rothstein. When, inevitably, some men refused to repay the loan, Rothstein used muscle. Monk Eastman, head of one of the most powerful street gangs and a rival of Owney Madden, served as his "collector."

This was Rothstein's first racket—one that in years to come would develop into a billion-dollar business. Moneylending, of course, had been around since business intercourse began, but it was Rothstein who adapted it to modern conditions and made it a part of the national economy.

Arnold "the Brain" Rothstein, "King of the Gamblers."

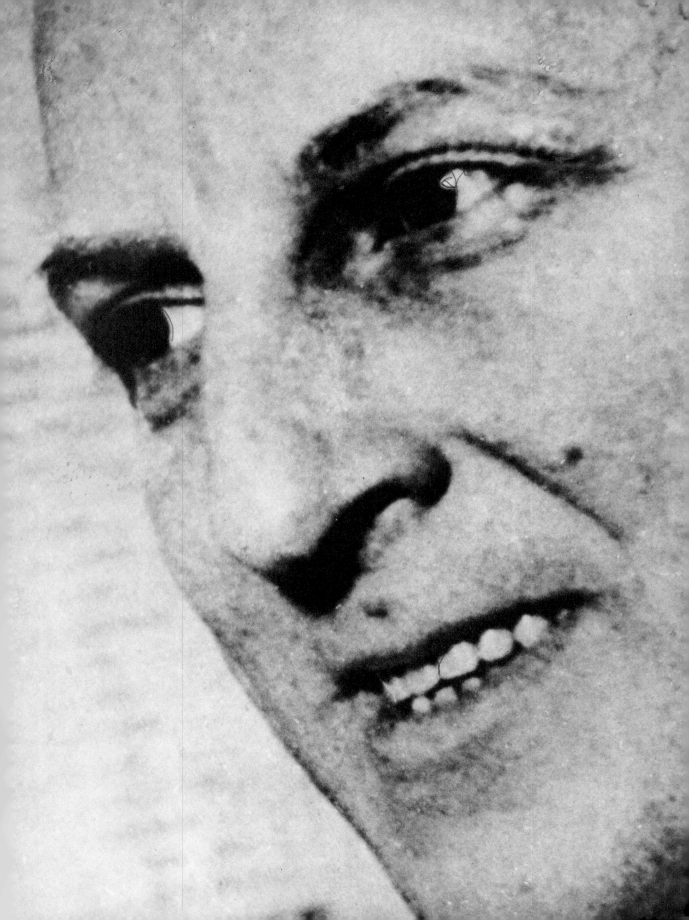

In 1971, the Senate Permanent Investigation Subcommittee, headed by Senator John McClellan, made a lot of noise about a "new" racket—the theft of valuable securities from Wall Street brokerage houses. Arnold Rothstein developed that racket in 1918.

Highly negotiable Liberty Bonds were the targets in the last year of the First World War. Messenger boys carrying them from brokerage house to bank were slugged on the street and robbed. Or some of them were. Police soon suspected that a "mastermind" had arranged for cooperation from a lot of the messengers. Evidence pointed to "Mr. Arnold," and as the thefts added up to millions pressure increased for an arrest.

Rothstein, who by now had bought a lot of protection, managed to shift the blame to Jules W. Arndt Stein, husband of Broadway star Fanny Brice and known to the press and police as Nicky Arnstein. At the last minute he tipped Nicky to get out of town.

Arnstein fled to Cleveland, known even then as a "safe town" for hoods. And for perhaps the first time the shadow of future organization became visible. Two mysterious money men who, in years to come, would act as bankers for the Cleveland Syndicate were disclosed to be involved with the New Yorkers in the disposal of the stolen Liberty Bonds. Sam Haas, formerly an associate of Tom McGinty in the newspaper-circulation wars, and Haas's associate in various deals, E. P. Strong, were the Clevelanders named. New York police charged bitterly that "influential politicians in Cleveland were closely connected with the confederates of Arnstein in the disposal of upward of $2 million worth of stolen securities." That New York politicians were in cahoots with Rothstein in the theft of the securities wasn't mentioned.

Eventually, when he had covered himself, Rothstein provided $100,000 bond and his own lawyer, William J. Fallon, to represent the fugitive. Nicky came back to New York

Rothstein, the sure-thing gambler, was suspected of masterminding the million-dollar Liberty Bonds theft racket.

Lend *the way they* Fight

Buy Bonds *to your* UTMOST

Dapper Nicky Arnstein, husband of Ziegfeld star Fanny Brice, was convicted in the bond theft. While she stood by him and continued playing on Broadway, he went to Leavenworth, but served only 20 months. They were later divorced.

FOUR... FOR VICTORY, BUY BOND

to stand trial. While Miss Brice and Fallon waited for him to be released in a nearby bar, someone stole her car parked outside. The bartender wasn't cooperative until told that Miss Brice was under the protection of Arnold Rothstein. Then he hastened to the telephone. Fifteen minutes later the car was returned and Monk Eastman offered personal apologies. His boys hadn't known the owner was "a friend of A. R."

The missing Liberty Bonds continued to show up for years. Some appeared in England, Canada, and Cuba where they paid for shipments of illicit booze. Later, some appeared in France and Switzerland as payment for narcotics shipments. For Arnold Rothstein was to mastermind the beginning of the rum-running business and organize the international narcotics traffic after he quit the liquor trade.

Despite his solid achievements, however, he is perhaps best remembered as the man who "fixed" the 1919 World Series and almost killed organized baseball in the process. Over the years, how many college players have been corrupted, how many

39

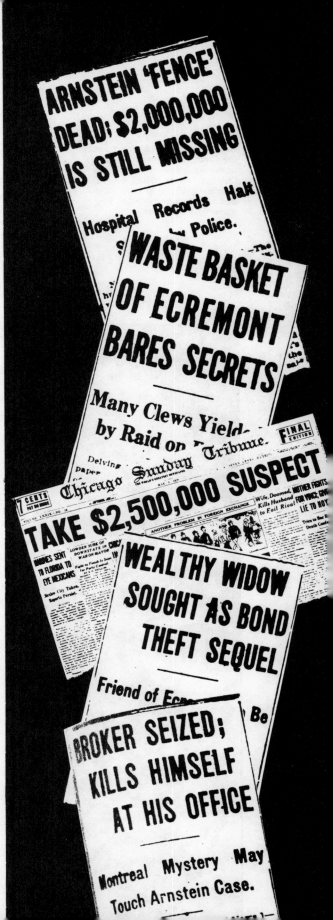

Going into the 1919 World Series, the Cincinnati Reds were 4–1 underdogs. When they beat the Chicago White Sox, everyone wondered why until eight White Sox players were indicted for throwing the series.

The players involved: top from left, Arnold "Chick" Gandil, Buck Weaver, Claude Williams, Eddie Cicotte; bottom from left, Oscar "Happy" Felsch, "Shoeless" Joe Jackson, Charles Risberg.

Below, ex-featherweight champion Abe Attell, accused of masterminding the plot. Arnold Rothstein, gambler and moneylender, denied he was involved.

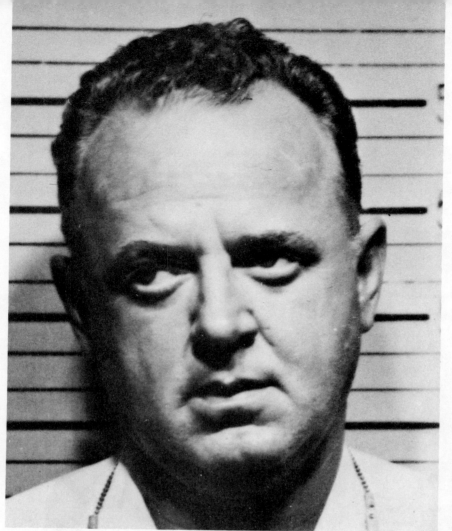

"Gil the Brain"
Beckley in 1959.

professional baseball, football, and basketball games have been fixed, how many fighters have taken "dives" will never be known. But it was Rothstein who started the racket. Ironically, when the National Football League set up protective machinery to guard against scandals in the late 1960s, its agents consulted the man generally conceded to be Rothstein's successor: Gilbert Lee Beckley, better known as "Gil the Brain." How much aid Beckley provided remains the NFL's secret, but so long as professional football teams remain "owned" by men with ties to organized crime, the league will need all the help it can get.

In sports betting, as in the other rackets with which he was to be identified, Rothstein but showed the way, but opened the door to potential profits surpassing anything dreamed of in the past. That other young Americans were quick to take advantage of Rothstein's breakthroughs was to be expected. America was indeed the Promised Land, and Prohibition was to provide the first big payoff.

2 THE BIG CHANCE

"The law approving Prohibition was enacted on January 1, 1920. Before the law was put into effect I predicted that a bottle of whiskey would bring in a large sum of money. I implored all my friends in Pittsburgh and the surrounding communities to store the whiskey where they stored their fruit and that I would pay them seventy-five cents a bottle. I established an agreement with Peppino Lonardo [Joseph Lonardo] of Cleveland, Ohio, to arrange for the storage on large farms some loads of whiskey that I had ordered. Since Peppino Lonardo was the capo of the Mafia in Cleveland, no farmer would refuse to grant him that favor.

"As soon as the Prohibition law was enforced to a greater extent, I found out that I had hit the mark because the law of supply and demand, as in similar circumstances, went into effect, that is, when the supply decreased the demand increased. The price of a bottle soared to $10. According to my figures from the amount of bottles I had in storage, I estimated their value as being in the hundreds of thousands of dollars. . ."

In such rambling fashion did Nicola Gentile describe the coming of Prohibition and the big chance it offered him and all others willing to break "man's law" to get rich quick.

Contrary to some popular assumptions, the law did not sneak up on anyone. The National Prohibition party was organized in 1869 in Chicago, and as early as 1876 it advocated that national prohibition be achieved by means of a constitutional amendment. A month after the United States entered the war in 1917, Congress banned the sale of liquor to men in uniform. By December, 1917, Congress had approved submission of the Eighteenth Amendment prohibiting liquor sales to the various states. By January, 1919, the necessary thirty-six states had ratified the Amendment. The Volstead Act, setting up legal machinery to enforce the constitutional ban on liquor, was passed by Congress over the veto of President Woodrow Wilson. The Amendment and the Act became effective on January 16, 1920. By no coincidence, the government chose that day to distribute more than four million bronze victory medals to all who had seen

JUST ONE PATCH AFTER ANOTHER.

—Halladay in the Providence *Journal*.

wartime military service.

The passage of restrictive legislation was made possible by a wave of idealism inspired by President Wilson's dream of a world without war. In comparison, "an era of efficient sobriety" seemed a modest goal indeed.

If "dry forces" had been lucky in the idealistic, get-things-done-now mood of the country during the drive to ban liquor, they were unfortunate in the attitude existing when the time came to enforce the anti-liquor laws. For reaction had begun, a turning-away from duty and high purpose to a personal search for private profit and pleasure. Not only did the new climate make a farce of the Anti-Saloon League's dream of voluntary compliance, but it contributed to the defeat

of Wilson's hopes for the League of Nations.

Leaders and lawmakers assumed the American people would obey the new law whether they liked it or not just as they paid income taxes. Effective enforcement without the cooperation of the public was as impossible as would be the enforcement of today's laws against narcotics if a majority of citizens abruptly decided they had a divine right to become drug addicts. The borders of the country stretched for 18,700 miles, offering smugglers a choice of unguarded land, sea, and air routes by which to bring in their illicit cargoes. Then there were built-in loopholes. Thousands of druggists could sell liquor on doctors' prescriptions, and plenty of druggists and doctors could be bribed or

The Chicago Daily Tribune.
THE WORLD'S GREATEST NEWSPAPER

FINAL EDITION

VOLUME LXXIX. NO. 1. C. [COPYRIGHT: 1920 BY THE TRIBUNE COMPANY] THURSDAY, JANUARY 1. 1920.—40 PAGES. THIS PAPER CONSISTS OF TWO SECTIONS—SECTION ONE ★ PRICE TWO CENTS IN CHICAGO AND SUBURBS. ELSEWHERE THREE CENTS

920 ARRIVES WET:

CAFES BECOME BOOZE CAFETERIAS

TO DEPORT RED LEADERS REDS SOON

Palmer Pledges War and Activity of Bolsheviki.

ARTHUR SEARS HENNING

ASKS AMERICA "TO SAVE WORLD WITH BIG LOAN"

New York, Dec. 31.—[Special]—Sir George Paish, former editor of the Statist and an English financial expert, arrived today on the Nieuw Amsterdam to discuss the international financial situation with bankers with a view to raising further loans and to improve the exchange rate.

He took a pessimistic view of the outlook for Europe, and he said that the United States was the only country which was able to supply a remedy for existing conditions.

"England, Sir George said, "is the financial clearing house for the whole of Europe, yet for that reason has in turn to be the first

PARTY CAUCUS ON CONVENTION BREEDS STRIFE

G. O. P. Chiefs at War Over Issuance of Call.

Sensational developments arise over the question of holding a caucus of the Republican delegates preliminary to the organization

TUMULTY DENIES WILSON LETTER AS TO CANDIDACY

Washington, D. C., Dec. 31.—[Special]—Denial was made today that President Wilson would write a letter announcing he was not a candidate for reelection, to be read at the Jackson day dinner on Jan. 8. Joseph P. Tumulty told friends that there was nothing in the report which was printed here this morning. Tumulty had a talk with the president early today, though it is not known whether this subject was mentioned.

This is not taken to mean that the president will be a candidate—only that he declines at this time to eliminate

BRITISH YEOMEN WIN LAND LOST FOR CENTURIES

Overlords Will Sell Millions of Acres of Estates.

BY JOHN S. STEELE
[Chicago Tribune Foreign News Service.]

Big Cities Forget Dry Law in Greeting 1920

NEW YORK, Dec. 31.—[New York the entry of the year that is now on its way has never been excelled in brilliance and spontaneous celebration. Finery was everywhere as thousands began taking their places around the table in the glistening restaurants of the Waldorf-Astoria, the Ritz Carlton, Astor Plaza, and Vanderbilt hotels.

From 8 o'clock in the evening until the gun crew there was life and gladness and revelry.

Broadway thundered with the peculiar feeling of those who dined and drank within her

WASHINGTON, D.C., Dec. 31.—[Special.]—"1920 Year 1919," who built the great American war wagons, rode to his doom in Washington tonight in a fireside charted, amid scenes of sparkling, splashing gayety.

Although it was in Washington that the old year issued his warthful and all-time prohibition decrees, he was far too far gone tonight to enforce them in the letter by parties to reform them in the letter. In one fashionable hotel waiters who had gone enough were seen to be tipped from the champagne bottles of the old undergraduate

NURSE HUSKY NEW YEAR BABE ON HIP FLASK

Bring Own Liquor to Loop in Grips and Even Trunks.

BY PERCY HAMMOND

The services of the night, mark Chicago's greeting in 1920, were as usual. That part of the ceremony which is performed in the

The New Year may have come in wet, but 16 days later the era of promised aridity arrived. Below, police smash up J. J. Kelley's drug store in Seattle, formerly a liquor store, which had been converted only halfheartedly.

otherwise persuaded. Prescriptions could be forged or stolen. The manufacture of industrial alcohol could be diverted to the production of illicit booze. It was still legal to make near beer. One had to brew real beer and then remove the alcohol—a circumstance with great and obvious potential. Finally, there was home-brewing and distilling. Hillbillies had been doing it since before the Whiskey Rebellion. It was practical; and on a large scale, it was impossible to police.

Despite the odds, however, Prohibition could have been a "noble experiment," tolerated for a few years and eventually discarded. No one has even today suggested that the desire for booze is as basic as the sex drive—as gamblers will say on behalf of their business at every opportunity. Had the American people in 1920 elected to office a responsible, dedicated, honest group of officials capable of establishing a moral and ethical tone, things might have taken a different course. Instead, the voters, riding a wave of reaction, elected Warren Harding and his "Ohio Gang." In search of "normalcy," the new administration made

exploitation and chicanery respectable.

How many citizens felt a need to obey the Prohibition law when it was common knowledge that President Harding had his official bootlegger, Elias Mortimer, and that liquor was served in the White House as well as in the famous "Little Green House on K Street" where the Ohio Gang made its deals in whiskey, oil, pardons, sheets for beds in Veterans Administration hospitals, and anything else in demand? The informed citizen thought none the less of his President upon learning of his drinking; it was the law he held in contempt.

And inevitably, when each citizen is allowed to decide which laws he will obey, there develops a contempt for other laws which seem to restrict a man's right to make a lot of fast bucks. "The business of the country is business" was a boast, not an apology.

In an era of growing cynicism and declining moral standards, the art of ballyhoo developed rapidly. As ancient Romans were diverted from official corruption by the pleasure of watching a lion devour a Christian, so Americans found escape in watching and

An anti-Prohibition parade on July 4, 1921.

Chicago Daily Tribune.
THE WORLD'S GREATEST NEWSPAPER

E LXXIX—NO. 264. C.   (COPYRIGHT 1920 BY THE CHICAGO TRIBUNE)   WEDNESDAY, NOVEMBER 3, 1920.—30 PAGES.   THIS PAPER CONSIST OF TWO SECTIONS—SECTION ONE   ★ ★ PRICE TWO CENTS IN CHICAGO

HARDING BY MILLIONS
G. O. P. TRIUMPHS IN CITY, STATE AND NATION

WINS;
MAY BE
F MILLION

ounty in the
es G. O. P.

HARDING VICTOR IN NEW YORK BY OVER A MILLION

All Records Broken by Empire State.

BULLETIN.

NEW YORK, Nov. 2.—Returns from 5,586 districts out of 7,306 in the state give Harding 1,498,934; Cox, 648,445. At this rate Harding will carry the state by 1,125,000. Returns from 2,514 districts gave:
302,580 W, Wadsworth, 535,-
Senator

CONGRESS, FOR GOOD MEASURE, SAFELY G. O. P.

12 Margin in Senate, 88 in House.

BY GRAFTON WILCOX

BULLETINS

The Illinois results on president and governor are indicated by the following table, worked out on an average lead per precinct as shown by the actual precincts heard from at 3 a.m.

HARDING'S LEAD

Chicago 625 of 2,210 pcts. ...247...60
Downstate, 866 of 3,357 pcts. ...442...862

Total ....785...922
County towns, 48 of 243 pcts. ...34...24

SMALL'S LEAD

Chicago 625 of 2,210 pcts. ...159...720
Downstate, 742 of 3,257 pcts. ...381...049

Total ....550...789
Grand total ....819...244

COUNTY G. O. P. SLATE ROMPS IN 200,000 VICTOR

Crowe by 210,000,
Righeimer 205,000.

COUNTY TICKET WINNERS

	VOTE FOR PRESIDENT					
STATES.	Electoral Vote.		DOUBTFUL	PLURALITIES. (Incomplete returns.)		
				1920.		1916.
	Harding	Cox		HARDING	COX	Wilson and Hughes
Alabama		12	3		60,000	76,600 W
Arizona						12,646 H
Arkansas	13	9			65,000	65,000 W
California				200,000		3,806 W
Colorado	6			20,000		76,508 W
Connecticut	7			75,000		6,728 H
Delaware	3			12,000		1,258 H
Florida		6			40,000	41,373 W
Georgia		14			100,000	120 W
Idaho	4					

COX AND LEAG
BURIED UND
HUGE MAJOR

South Alone Cli
to Democracy

BY ARTHUR SEARS HEN

Harding and Cox

President Harding and his cabinet. From left, standing, Albert M. Fall, Secy. of the Interior; Will Hays, Postmaster General; Harry M. Daugherty, Atty. General; Henry C. Wallace, Secy. of Agriculture; Herbert Hoover, Secy. of Commerce; James J. Davis, Secy. of Labor; seated, John W. Weeks, Secy. of War; Andrew Mellon, Secy. of the Treasury; Charles Evans Hughes, Secy. of State; President Harding; Vice-President Calvin Coolidge; Edwin Denby, Secy. of the Navy.

48

George Remus, who gave up a lucrative law practice to take up bootlegging, was one of the most successful illicit liquor dealers in the country. He is shown here in 1927 upon winning his freedom after his trial for killing his wife. He was judged insane.

talking about Babe Ruth, Red Grange, or Jack Dempsey. It was the age of the con man. It was a time to believe everything and believe in nothing—except, of course, the God-given possibility that tomorrow or next week you would hit it lucky and get rich.

As far as crime was concerned, there were four stages of Prohibition. The first, as Gentile's action indicates, entailed getting the most for the liquor on hand, in stock. Millions of gallons were available if ways could be found to introduce them into commerce. The key in many cases (many thousands of cases) was a legal instrument known as a "permit for withdrawal." It allowed the lucky person holding the permit to withdraw whiskey from bonded warehouses where it was stored. Officially the whiskey withdrawn had to be used for medicinal purposes. Since the owner of the whiskey could not sell his supply in any other way, he naturally didn't look too closely when an individual holding a permit for withdrawal appeared with money to buy.

Perhaps the biggest operator of this type

to appear was George Remus, known as the "gentle grafter" and "quiet corruptor." He was born in Germany in 1873 and brought to Chicago by his parents three years later. Intensely ambitious, he studied pharmacy and at nineteen obtained a license by swearing he was two years older. While working as a pharmacist, he studied law and soon was admitted to the bar. In the next two decades he won a reputation as a criminal lawyer. With the advent of Prohibition he saw a chance to combine his two careers—his knowledge of pharmacy and his ability as a criminal lawyer. Selling his law books, he moved to Cincinnati, the geographical center of the distilling industry, with about $100,000 in cash. Remus went into business on a huge scale. Over a two-year period he sold $70 million worth of bonded whiskey. In testimony before a Senate investigating committee in 1924, he explained how simple it was:

"I would organize drug companies and wholesale drug companies and obtain permits. That gave you the privilege of

withdrawing alcoholic liquors from distilleries or bonded warehouses pursuant to the Volstead law. . . It is, of course, upon those withdrawals [the permits] being issued, legally issued, that the liquor could be sold. For those institutions [the drug companies] I paid $50,000 to $325,000 for each one of them."

It also proved simpler, he said, to buy the distilleries and their warehouses. He could remember owning seven in 1924, and there might have been more. From the bonded warehouses booze was diverted in railroad-car lots.

It wasn't all profit, of course. In order to operate it was necessary to buy the withdrawal permits from federal officials or, to put it exactly, to bribe public officials to issue the permits. It was necessary to buy "protection" from local authorities. Remus estimated he spent $20 million in bribes and completely corrupted the official life of three states—Ohio, Kentucky, and Indiana—in the process. Decades after a reform drive cleaned up Cincinnati, its Kentucky suburbs remained vice dens and illegal gambling centers. Remus was responsible for much of this.

On the federal level, Remus dealt directly with the Ohio Gang in Washington. His contact was with Jess Smith, a crony of both President Harding and Attorney General Harry Daugherty. Eventually Smith would kill himself or, some said, be killed to protect Harding. Remus would testify against Daugherty when the stink became too strong to ignore.

Remus won the title "King of the Bootleggers," and for a time he lived like a king in a mansion overlooking the Ohio River. The house cost over a million dollars, furnished with costly paintings and art objects from Europe. The doorknobs were gold, as were the fixtures in the bathroom. In this palace on Price Hill Remus installed his queen, Imogene, and in her honor he held parties

Attorney General Harry Daugherty, at right, and his man Friday, Jess Smith.

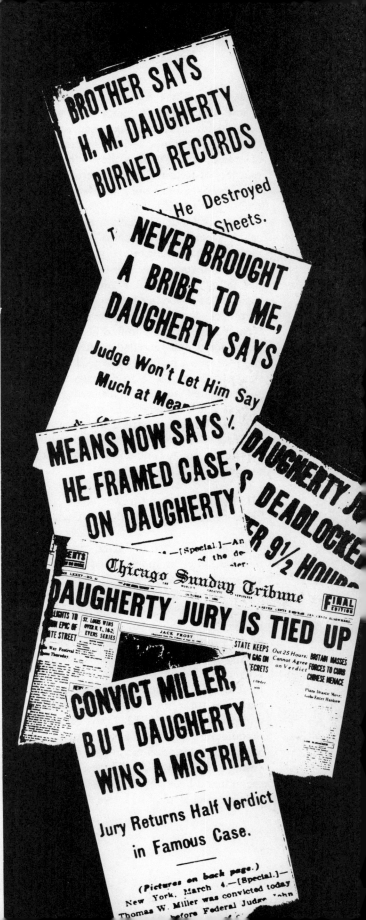

that put those of the fictional Gatsby to
shame. Guests at one dinner party were pre-
sented with expensive motor cars as favors.
Only the best liquor and food were served,
of course, and "Death Valley"—the headquarters of Remus's liquor operations outside
Cincinnati—seemed very far away. Then,
one day, the roof fell in.

Unbribed federal agents from other states
raided Death Valley. Remus was indicted
and eventually went to prison. When released
he found divorce papers waiting. Imogene
had fallen in love with a federal agent
assigned to probe her husband's affairs.
Heartsick, for he had truly loved his wife,
Remus hurried home to find his palace had
been looted. Imogene had carried off everything of value, including the gold doorknobs.
And now Remus's despair changed to rage.

He located Imogene and one day trailed
her car into Cincinnati's Eden Park where he
shot her to death. Charged with murder, he
pleaded not guilty by reason of insanity and
was acquitted. A Cincinnati newspaper commented:

He did his bit, and threw a fit.
Had he been poor, the electric chair for sure.

Remus remarried and lived quietly for
decades, an elder statesman of crime. The
corruption he had created lived after him.

Remus was King of the Bootleggers, but
Abraham Auerbach was more typical of
the hundreds who got rich during Phase One
of the Prohibition era. Along with his brother
Louis, he came to the United States in 1900,
and reached the Woodland district of Cleveland in 1906. Along the way they learned the
barbering trade, and they opened barber shops
and prospered. By 1912, Louis began to
manufacture hair tonic and Abraham bought
a furniture store and made friends of many
young couples by his willingness to sell them
secondhand beds and bureaus on credit.

It was the alcohol in Louis's "Love Me,

54

Gaston B. Means, henchman for the Ohio Gang, who claimed in 1930 that he arranged for the collection of graft from bootleggers for federal protection.

NAVY HASN'T
GUN TO FIGHT,
CHIEF SAYS

ust Skirmish;
's to Come.

June 3.—[Spe.
d has not yet be.

into be
om

M SCHOONER
ATES SEIZED
FIGHT AT SEA

Miquelon, June 3.—
in irons, the French
rts II. is being towed
after a chase and
eas rivaling the
nish main.
tured at mid-
twelve hour
am trawler
rail when
, N. S.
five of
the
were
ns.
ch

Prohibition, said the nation's press, made the bootlegger a vicious and corrupting influence in American life. At right, a house in East Detroit is raided; 132 barrels of fermenting mash were found.

Dearie" hair tonic and toilet water that opened the door to wealth with the coming of Prohibition. In 1922, in the first major alcohol diversion case of many to come, the Auerbach brothers were charged with diverting nearly $1 million worth of alcohol from the production of hair tonic to the manufacture of booze. Both men went to prison. Abraham made good of his time by learning to write English, which he did so well that friends in high places persuaded President Calvin Coolidge to commute his sentence. Abraham then went back to Cleveland, tangled with some moonshiners, and was convicted of murdering them. Returned to prison and assigned to the prison barber shop, Auerbach eventually cut his throat with a razor.

The same sort of thing, of course, was going on in states other than Ohio. Jacob Stein, a disbarred New York attorney who was to play a curious role in the evolution of organized crime, has given some insight as to how it worked. In sworn testimony, he described his meeting with Gaston B. Means, a friend and close associate of William J. Burns, then head of the Bureau of Investigation. The meetings took place in New York in November, 1922. On one occasion, according to Stein:

"Means said he had been promised by Mr. Willian J. Burns that within a day or two thereafter there would be established a department to be known as the Prohibition Unit of the Department of Justice and that he would have full charge of said department [unit] and that he would be in a position to release liquor from any bonded warehouse

or distillery in this country, and that he desired me, if possible, to line up for him various distilleries who were desirous of releasing liquor.

"He stated that the price for releasing liquor would be $200 per barrel, and that I was to receive my share from the distilleries, or from anybody who desired to release liquor, as this $200 was to be divided in four equal ways: $50 going to William J. Burns, $50 going to the Attorney General, $50 to the Republican Campaign Committee, and $50 was his share. He also stated that the price on case goods would be $20 per case. He stated to me that in removing liquor from these different warehouses or distilleries, that if the parties desired to have the liquor removed by government trucks, it would cost them $50 per barrel, and government

trucks would deliver the liquor to its permanent destination."

That Means was an accomplished liar cannot be doubted, but it is a matter of record that Burns appointed him a special agent and that he was close to Daugherty and even to President Harding. Nor is there any question that such deals as Stein described were made by high officials and ranking members of the Ohio Gang. Means was on a first-name relationship with J. Edgar Hoover, then assistant director of the Bureau of Investigation, although Hoover's apologists—benefiting by hindsight—have since insisted that Hoover really didn't like Means.

With such cooperation on the federal level, it isn't surprising that existing stocks of whiskey and alcohol were soon depleted. The second phase of Prohibition began—the manufacture of rot-gut in hundreds of thousands of small stills throughout the country.

Anyone was free to make liquor, and not a great deal of money was needed to get started. One could also sell as he pleased. The situation, however, was made to order for those individuals possessing sufficient wealth or muscle to move in and "organize" the business in specific localities. Leaders of the various Mafia "families" were in such a position.

Development along community lines was the pattern, and in large cities the slum areas were segregated on ethnic lines. Capos, accustomed to running affairs of the Italian-Sicilian ghettos, had little difficulty in taking control of that phase of the home-brew business. The distiller needed help in getting raw material, in marketing, in buying freedom from police interference. This the capo could supply.

In some cities such as Chicago warfare developed between bosses of rival ethnic gangs. In Detroit, rival Jewish gangs fought to death, while in Cleveland civil war raged within the Mafia.

In Chicago, Johnny Torrio was one of several important gang leaders operating independently of the Mafia. A Brooklyn import, he won power by arranging for his uncle, white-slaver Jim Colosimo, to be murdered five months after the Volstead Act went into effect. While retaining an interest in prostitution and gambling, Torrio turned to the beer and liquor business using his string of taverns and brothels as a base. In the summer of 1920, Torrio held a series of conferences with leaders of other gangs, persuading them to abandon other rackets in favor of bootlegging. An astute businessman first and foremost, Torrio also made deals with respectable citizens, and took charge of breweries owned by them. He also moved to control the output of thousands of small stills being independently operated.

Gangster chieftain Johnny Torrio. An opera devotee, he neither smoked nor drank, was never heard to utter a profane or obscene word.

Said Al Capone, "When I sell liquor, it's bootlegging. When my patrons serve it on silver trays on Lake Shore Drive, it's hospitality." A great popular hero, by 1927 his net profit was conservatively estimated at $60 million a year, mostly from selling liquor. In 1931 he was convicted of income tax evasion. He is seen here on the train en route to prison.

With fairly effective control of the supply, Torrio was able to form alliances with other gangs who were primarily concerned with distribution to retail outlets. The entire area of Cook County, including Chicago, was divided into "territories," and for a brief period there was peace and prosperity. Since Torrio was preoccupied with high-level matters, he let Al Capone handle such muscle work as was occasionally necessary.

"Scarface Al" Capone was a pudgy punk born in Brooklyn, New York, in 1899. He attended school on Adams Street with another youth destined to be the notorious Lucky Luciano. Indeed, Capone considered Luciano a second cousin. Both boys came under the influence of Torrio, seventeen years older than Capone and boss of a well-known street gang. Torrio maintained his New York contacts after answering his uncle's call to Chicago, and when he needed a reliable enforcer he sent for Capone. Under investigation for murder in Brooklyn, Al was glad to go west. Torrio put him to work first as a bouncer in a brothel and then let him take on greater responsibilities as vice-president in charge of enforcement.

Capone modeled himself after the new strong man of Italy, Benito Mussolini. He loved the good life: women, food, liquor, diamonds, and silk underwear. He enjoyed flattery and generously rewarded those who provided it. When crossed, however, he became hysterical with rage and was reported to have battered the brains out of several of his boys with a baseball bat upon deciding they had betrayed him.

Such a man of violence was useful to Torrio, who enjoyed the exercise of power rather than its trappings. A capacity for direct action was respected more than the ability to plan, and to maintain the loyalty of his "troops" Torrio had to command fear and respect. At the height of his power he gave orders—through Capone—to about seven hundred gangsters of whom 95 percent were

Johnny Torrio, objecting to having his picture taken, races out into the street to pick up a brick to throw at the photographer.

of foreign birth: about six hundred and thirty
Italian-Sicilians, seventy-five Jews, and
thirty-seven Irish. Despite their smaller
numbers, the Jews and Irish were represented
on the executive level by men like Jake
"Greasy Thumb" Guzik and Murray "the
Camel" Humphreys who held posts of high
rank, which is perhaps but another reason
why a man like Capone was needed to keep
the rank-and-file troops in line.

The conquest of Cicero, a suburb west of
Chicago, but in its own right the fifth largest
city in Illinois, was perhaps the best example
of Torrio diplomacy backed by Capone
terror. Late in 1923, after a series of moves
on his chessboard, Torrio forced the racket
bosses of the West Side—the two O'Donnell
brothers, Myles and Klondike—to accept a
peace treaty. The deal of course depended
upon political control of the city remaining
in the hands of friendly politician Eddie
Vogel, who also operated slot machines on
the side.

Vogel dominated the city's government
which, officially, was headed by Mayor
Joseph Z. Klenha. Early in 1924, when the
Democrats put up a serious challenge to
Klenha, Capone mobilized his troops and
moved into town to make sure the citizens
voted Republican. Pitched battles developed.
Belatedly, Chicago police were deputized
and rushed to Cicero in a vain effort to
restore democracy. In one battle, the police
killed Frank Capone, Al's brother, but that
proved small comfort to good citizens when
the ballots were counted. The Mob-backed
Klenha won an overwhelming victory, and
Cicero remained "a walled City of the Syndicate" for forty years. Successive Republican
administrations tried to give the city a better
image by boasting it was the "best lighted" in
the country, and arranging for "respectable"
places to close in time for honest employees
and customers to get off the streets before
the Mob-owned joints opened for the night.
Wide streets and parks gave Cicero the

Al Capone's city, Cicero, ILL., in 1928.

CHICAGO HISTORICAL SOCIETY

CHICAGO HISTORICAL SOCIETY

CICERO'S PLIGHT AS VICTIM OF GANG REVEALED

Officials Intimidated by Vice Chieftains.

CICERO TO SHOW WORLD THAT IT DISDAINS GUNMEN

Pastor Heads Drive to Clear Town's Name.

CAPONE BREWERY RUNNING ONLY 5 DAYS IS RAIDED

Destroy

GUNMEN
BULLETS

NEW GANG MACHINE GUN AY ON CAPONI

Seeks Control of Gambling, Police Say.

Earl "Hymie" Weiss, leader of the North Side Gang, declared war on Torrio and Capone. One day as Torrio and his wife returned home from shopping, two gunmen rushed across the street. Bullets riddled the car; the chauffeur was wounded, and Torrio fell with five slugs in his jaw, arm, abdomen and chest, while Mrs. Torrio watched in horror.

appearance of an all-American city, but Capone's successors ran it nonetheless.

Despite the victory in Cicero, trouble was brewing on the North Side of Chicago, the "territory" of Irish gangster Dion O'Banion and his cohorts. O'Banion complained to Torrio that the six Genna brothers were flooding his territory with homegrown rot-gut whiskey which they sold for half the price O'Banion got for his better-grade stuff. The Genna boys were Sicilians, proud, ignorant, treacherous, and devoutly religious. They went to church regularly and carried rosaries in their pistol pockets. Their whiskey was produced in hundreds of corn-sugar stills located in tenement houses in the Taylor Street district of the West Side. Gross sales were estimated at $350,000 a month, and the whole operation was protected by Torrio. When O'Banion's complaints got no action, the Irishman acted on his own. He hijacked a Genna truck. Only intervention by Mike Merlo, the highly respected capo of Chicago, prevented the Gennas from declaring war immediately. Merlo was one of the few Mafia leaders who seemed more concerned with the humanitarian aspects of the Honored Society's code than with its tradition of blood and terror. When he died on November 8, 1924, his successor was Angelo Genna. Two days later, O'Banion, who had declared "them Sicilians" could go to hell—was murdered in his flower shop.

The alliance put together by Torrio began to fall apart. Early in 1925, Torrio was wounded by gunmen under the command of Hymie Weiss (Wajciechowski), who had succeeded O'Banion as boss of the North Side. Chicago was just too uncivilized, decided Torrio, who upon his release from the hospital found safety by spending a few months in the Lake County jail on a minor charge. While still in jail, he formally turned over his entire empire to Capone. Freed, he left Chicago in disgust and took a long voyage to the Pacific while he waited for the times to

Mrs. Torrio, seen below coming from Jackson Park Hospital with Frank Ragen, its owner, would not help the police in finding the gunmen. "What good would it do?" she said. In the hospital Torrio, left, was guarded by gunmen under Capone's personal command.

Mike Merlo, influential and respected Mafia capo of Chicago, kept the peace between warring gangs. He died of natural causes in November, 1924; $100,000 worth of flowers were sent to his home, filling the house and the lawn outside. Most impressive was a 12-foot wax-and-flowers figure of Merlo, said to be a good likeness, carried in a car preceding the hearse. Twenty-five cars with flowers followed.

Dion O'Banion was leader of a gang which menaced the Torrio-Capone reign. On the day of Mike Merlo's funeral, three men entered O'Banion's florist shop. He carried three guns in specially tailored pockets, but this time he was off guard. He extended his hand. One man grasped it and held on while the other two pumped five bullets into his body and a sixth into his head. His funeral was the gaudiest of all gangland burials.

O'Banion's casket cost $10,000. His
body "lay in state" for three days
and was viewed by 40,000 people.
The funeral procession, a mile long,
was led by three bands and a police
escort from a neighboring town
(Chicago police were prohibited
from participating). Among the
baskets of flowers was one "From Al."

catch up with him. His wealth, estimated at $30 million, was sufficient, but his pleasure had never been in money alone. It was the exercise of power he enjoyed. Upon returning to New York, his first home, he found other men of the same persuasion, and he worked with them to help establish a national alliance of regional "combinations."

It is ironic that Torrio's reputation has been eclipsed over the years by that of his lieutenant. Capone, of course, was flashy, colorful, and vain. He loved publicity and courted it. The Chicago press gave him all he wanted—he made good copy which sold newspapers. Yet without the organization Torrio had painstakingly constructed over fifteen years, Capone would have been nothing but a punk. His attempt to capture by force what Torrio had failed to achieve by reason was, of course, doomed to failure. But a lot of people died in the process— some of them at the hands of Al himself— and the body count helped make him a legend in his lifetime. At the height of his power he controlled no more than a few suburban cities and perhaps one-fourth of Chicago, but that was enough to make him the most powerful animal in that particular jungle. Because of his national publicity, the Mafia relaxed its rules and admitted him—a non-Sicilian—to membership. But he never became capo of Chicago, and the organization bequeathed him by Torrio remained a "combination." It is still a combination today —the Chicago Syndicate—and the gang killings that have continued over the decades testify that it still lacks complete control. When a gang gets effective control, the killings stop. It is competition that makes gang murders on a large scale necessary.

In Chicago, individual gang leaders lived like feudal lords, each supreme in his own territory and each attempting to enlarge it at the expense of others. By virtue of Torrio's brains, Capone was for a time the most powerful, but he was unable to defeat a rather minor punk named Bugs Moran. His effort to eliminate Moran led to the St. Valentine's Day Massacre which, as much as anything else, inflated Capone's reputation. Seven men were lined up against the wall of a warehouse and mowed down with machine guns in that famous fiasco, but none of them was Moran. Approaching the trap, he had taken alarm and turned back at the last minute. Capone's killers, assuming he was there, fired at will and killed men who, if not innocent, were certainly not important enemies of the Boss. Capone, meanwhile, was sitting in the office of the Dade County solicitor in sunny Miami—a beautiful alibi. Moran lived on long after Capone died; it was lung cancer that finally killed him.

Perhaps Chicago was simply too large for one man or one organization to control. The New York metropolitan area was even larger, and the problem was more complex. Five Mafia "families" existed there along with ethnic gangs representing every sizable minority in the area: Jews, Irish, Chinese, Syrians, Greeks, Poles, Negroes, and others. Not only were there struggles for power within each gang, but wars between gangs were common. The area was so large, containing so much wealth and so many people, that later is was possible to argue there was enough for everyone. In the early stages, however, no one even attempted to bring order out of the chaos. Thus there was no opportunity for a Torrio at this stage of development and no need for an enforcer like Capone.

It wasn't until Arnold Rothstein turned "Legs" Diamond loose as a hijacker that a trend toward centralization began.

John T. Noland was Diamond's real name, an unsentimental Irishman, who began working for Rothstein as a muscle man in 1919. In 1921, Diamond organized a gang financed and protected by Rothstein to steal booze—and furs, narcotics, and anything else handy—from the thousands of small

George "Bugs" Moran, new chief of the North Side Gang, established his headquarters in a garage at 2122 North Clark Street. On St. Valentine's Day, 1929, six of his gang and an optometrist friend, who liked to "play around" with gangsters, were in the garage waiting for a shipment of liquor. A touring car pulled up; five men, three in police uniform, got out and entered the garage. They disarmed the Moran men, lined them up facing the wall, and sprayed them with machine-gun bullets. One of the killers then shot every man with a pistol as he lay on the floor. Bugs Moran escaped by a few minutes. Approaching the garage and seeing the supposed policemen, he thought it was a raid and stayed clear.

Frank Gusenberg
crawled 20 feet
toward the door with
14 bullets in him. He
died in the hospital
and told the police
nothing. Picture
above shows the
bodies being taken
out. At right, Bugs
Moran, who said,
"Only the Capone
gang kills like that."

operators who lacked the organization and
the funds necessary for physical protection.
So successful was he that he attracted to his
gang such volunteers as Charles Luciano,
later known as Lucky Luciano, and Arthur
Flegenheimer, better known as Dutch
Schultz.

Action breeds reaction, and the raids of
Diamond provided opportunity for another
individual who would do more than anyone
else to put organized crime—at this stage
still struggling to be born—on an efficient,
sophisticated basis. Meyer Lansky, an expert
auto mechanic and friend of Luciano, formed
what became known as the Bugs and Meyer
Mob with Benjamin "Bugsy" Siegel. It began
as an auto rental agency, and developed into
a crack corps of gunmen who for a price
would protect liquor cargoes or, for another
price, hijack a rival's supply. The group
served as a forerunner of Murder, Inc.

In 1971, from a vantage point in Israel,
Lansky was to look back on his youth and
claim the Bugs and Meyer Mob was just a
group of Jewish boys he organized to protect
other Jewish boys from the brutal Irish gangs
of the period. At the time he made that statement, however, Lansky was fighting an
attempt to expel him from Israel and was
trying to prove his devotion to Jews in every
possible way. Actually, Lansky's genius was
in bridging ethnic gulfs. His friendship with
Lucky Luciano was one of the most
important relationships in the evolution of
organized crime. Similarly, he was able to
work with Paul "the Waiter" Ricca, successor
to Torrio-Capone in Chicago, with Joe
Massei and Peter Licavoli in Detroit, with
Frank Milano and Big Al Polizzi in
Cleveland. He got along with the Irish too, as
his association with them on the docks of
New York and his friendship with such men
as Thomas McGinty and Sam Garfield
proves. Siegel and Lansky made a good team.
Siegel was taller than his friend, and several
years younger. Handsome, aggressive, he

Partners in the Bugs and Meyer
Mob: Benjamin "Bugsy" Siegel and
Meyer Lansky.

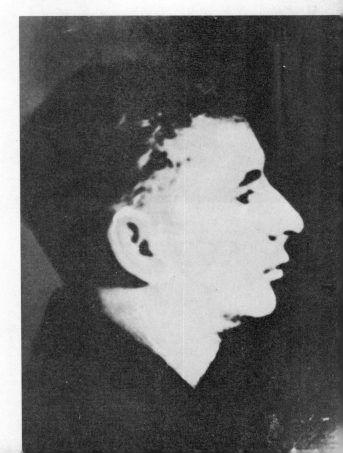

Meyer Lansky, main architect of
organized crime.

"Big Joe" Lonardo supplied so many stills to Italians in the Cleveland ghetto that the odor of fermenting mash hung over the whole section 24 hours a day.

loved action and the spotlight whereas Lansky enjoyed the shadows. For years Bugsy carried out Lansky's orders; it was only when he tried to think for himself that he got into trouble and was executed by the syndicate for insubordination. The Flamingo Hotel and Casino remains in Las Vegas as a monument to his memory.

But we are getting ahead of our history.

By 1924, rumrunning had become the third stage of Prohibition in New York, and while rot-gut continued to be produced in thousands of Mafia-controlled stills, it ceased to be a major industry as far as money and political influence were concerned. Rothstein withdrew his support of Diamond, and his gang dissolved. Ironically, however, Legs outlived his benefactor by almost three years. An outlaw among outlaws, he enjoyed violence for its own sake. Unwittingly he served as the wolf whose savagery forces the sheep to huddle together under the protection of a shepherd.

In Cleveland, meanwhile, the manufacture of rot-gut became centered in the Woodland district where it came under the control of the Lonardo brothers. "Big Joe" Lonardo, who weighed about three hundred pounds, came to Cleveland around 1900 and opened a store. His brothers, John and Frank, soon joined him, and by Prohibition they were prosperous and powerful figures in the ghetto. They got into the booze business by their control of corn sugar, an essential ingredient, and soon installed the logical twist known as the "commission house."

Thousands of Italian-Sicilians living in the slums of Woodland were equipped by the Lonardos with cheap stills and all necessary raw materials. They produced the rot-gut and turned it over to their benefactors to sell. For their labors, and the use of their homes, they received a commission on the profits. In many ways it resembled the share-cropping by which they had eked out a living in the rocky fields of Sicily, but the work wasn't so hard.

Prohibition turned many normally temperate beer drinkers into drinkers of whiskey, real or bogus.

Making home brew was a popular pastime. Stills came in all sizes and could be set up anywhere in the house.

For the Lonardos it was a chance to get immensely rich while at the same time winning the affection of thousands of new citizens who looked up to the brothers as padrones or godfathers. Unhappily, of course, it also attracted the jealous interest of other aggressive members of the Honored Society who saw no reason under "human law" why they shouldn't knock off their capo, Joe Lonardo, and get all the loot for themselves.

Intoxicated by all the new wealth suddenly available, the Mafia was in a state of strife unusual even for that vendetta-ridden organization. Nicola Gentile, the old "troubleshooter," has provided some insight into conditions that ultimately would bring civil war on a national scale.

Following his accumulation of sudden wealth by stockpiling booze on the eve of Prohibition, Gentile buckled under the strain and a Mafia doctor in Cleveland ordered him to get absolute rest. When news reached New York that he was in the hospital, everyone automatically assumed he had been shot. A friend, Umberto Valente, hastened to his bed to get details so a vendetta could be launched.

"Realizing that his suspicions were not correct," Gentile said, "Valente began worrying about the possibility someone would take advantage of my illness and try to surprise me."

Gentile decided to seek "additional rest and tranquility in Sicily" where he had married on a previous visit home and fathered a child. But unhappily, there was no peace to be found on his native shore. An Italian-American named Francesco La Paglia was shot and, before dying, named Gentile as his assassin. The visiting celebrity "had the wisdom to go into hiding."

While in hiding, Gentile was visited by a Mafia delegation from America led by Umberto Valente. In the group was Piddu "the Clutching Hand" Morello who had recently been deposed as capo di capi re by Toto D'Aquila. The excuse for replacing

Morello was rather logical—he had been sentenced to twenty-five years in federal prison. Naturally, D'Aquila wanted to safeguard his new position—he couldn't feel secure so long as Piddu was alive and free on appeal. After all, the courts of the United States being obsessed with such abstractions as justice and evidence, anything might happen. So Morello and all his close friends had been marked for death.

Valente, considered Morello's legitimate heir, was number one on the death list. He had a reputation as a dangerous and elusive man. "By his ferocity and the manner he was able to vanish after committing an exploit, he was nicknamed 'Lo Spirito,' the Ghost," Gentile explained.

The outlaws hoped Nicola would have enough influence to form a commission with power to convene a general assembly of the Mafia throughout the United States, and countermand Morello's death sentence. The Mafia, for all its reliance on force and terror, still clung to its internal machinery when all else failed. Gentile promised to try as soon as he could settle his personal problems. Six months later, he slipped back into the country at Boston but D'Aquila's spies were soon on his trail. Technically, under Mafia rules, Gentile was still under the protection of a Sicilian "family" since he transferred his membership there from Pittsburgh when he returned to Sicily. Such protection was of little value in America, however, so it was imperative that he join a powerful family in this country. He selected a Brooklyn family headed by Nicholas Schirio. He had long had a good relationship with Schirio. Moreover, the Brooklyn capo had adopted a neutral position in the quarrel between D'Aquila and Morello. Gentile obtained the necessary "nulla osta" (permission) from Sicily and "in this way I found peace of mind because nobody would be able to do away with my person."

Having achieved official standing, Gentile

"Big Tim" Murphy, shown with his wife and daughter, was the dean of the labor racketeers in Chicago in the 1920s. He served a term in the state legislature—and a term in the penitentiary for mail robbery. Allegedly it was Big Tim who coined the phrase "take a one-way ride," but it was Hymie Weiss who first put it into practice. Big Tim was killed in 1928. Below, an unknown victim of a "one-way ride."

The term "speakeasy" for an unlicensed saloon dates from 1900. During Prohibition it became a household word.

met secretly with Valente in Boston to discuss plans for forming the commission and then went on to Cleveland. Joe Lonardo, the capo, received him with honor and "took me to his newly built home in the construction of which he had spent in the neighborhood of $120,000. In the palatial home there was an apartment complete with all the comforts which Lonardo assigned to me. A few days later he took me to his store where he sold sugar of corn from which bootleggers extracted alcohol, then fermented and allowed to stagnate. In short, he sold everything necessary for the production of alcohol."

Although impressed with Lonardo's success, Gentile decided Big Joe "was under the diabolical impulses of Toto D'Aquila and saw his capo di capi re in such a light that he worshiped him like a God." Lonardo tried to bring Gentile around to the same attitude by presenting him with a $75,000 bank account. Gentile warned Lonardo not to display such wealth since D'Aquila maintained an army of secret agents to kill any capo who became rich and famous and thus a potential rival. Gentile finally despaired of his efforts to persuade Lonardo to help form a commission.

He later wrote: "I have to call attention to the fact that Lonardo, besides being illiterate, was slow-witted. The majority of the assembly of the Mafia was composed of such men who were considered in their cities of origin to be personalities but who in New York and hence in the assembly became but a number."

Salvatore Caldarone, capo of Pittsburgh, was willing to help get Morello's death sentences voided, but warned Gentile of making a public show of opposition to D'Aquila unless he had the strength to carry the day. In an effort to get that strength, Gentile went to Chicago to win the support of Mike Merlo, the respected capo of that city. Merlo commanded "a hundred select young men for which he was feared, and, therefore, was

Detroit agents "knock off" the second-largest still found in the area.

able to impose his will." But Merlo "had gone to Italy on a pleasure trip." When he returned, according to Gentile, he was shot down on a "corner of Chicago known as the 'Corner of the Dead.'"

"I informed Valente of the failure of my diplomatic mission and advised him to stay a long way from Cleveland," wrote Gentile afterward.

But the struggle within the Mafia continued. D'Aquila was soon murdered by the Valente-Gentile faction led by Joe "the Boss" Masseria, and the stage was set for all-out civil war.

During this time, Big Joe Lonardo and his brothers in Cleveland were facing a challenge from the seven Porello brothers. Gradually the Porellos wrested control of the corn-sugar business. On October 13, 1927, Big Joe accepted an invitation to talk business with the Porellos, and was shot to death in the rear of a Porello-owned barbershop. Ironically, he went to the meeting unguarded because two of his "hired companions," as the newspapers called them, had been picked up by police in connection with another murder. His brothers were also killed soon afterward. The Porellos were supreme. Joe Porello appointed himself capo of Cleveland,

and a grand council of the Mafia was called at the Hotel Statler on December 5, 1928, to confirm him. Someone tipped off the cops and the meeting was raided. Twenty-three men were arrested and ordered to get out of town and stay out. It was the first recorded meeting of the Mafia known to police officials in America, and like many that followed, it was a fiasco.

For rot-gut whiskey was now so rotten it created a demand for good liquor. When that demand was satisfied, few customers were left for the Mafia-dominated home-brew industry. Rumrunning, the third stage of Prohibition, required a new type of mind, international credit, and a unified effort that only a crime syndicate could provide. In Cleveland, a new group called the Mayfield Road Mob took over from the Porellos and survived by becoming allies of the rumrunners of the developing Cleveland Syndicate. In New York, new leaders brought the Mafia into a working alliance with "the Combination" which soon would become the Eastern Syndicate.

The Mafia had lost its big chance to dominate organized crime, but greater opportunities loomed for those men willing to forget the past in order to shape the future.

3 THE MELTING POT

Arnold "the Brain" Rothstein once told a newspaper reporter, "You want to know how I make my money? There are two million fools born for every intelligent man. That ought to answer you."

The third stage of Prohibition—rum-running—began in New York well ahead of the rest of the country for two major reasons. The metropolitan area was so large the demand for booze couldn't be satisfied by diversion or by home manufacture; and Rothstein operated in New York. Thanks largely to him, the first three stages of Prohibition happened simultaneously, although as time passed and syndicates organized, rumrunning became far and away the chief source of "the real McCoy."

It was "Big Maxey" Greenberg of Detroit who started the bottles rolling. He had been bringing in booze across Lake Erie almost from the start of Prohibition, but he lacked the funds to expand. He turned to an old buddy, Waxey Gordon (Irving Wexler). Waxey didn't have the cash either, but he knew someone who did and who was receptive to big-money ideas. Gordon had worked

for Rothstein in pre-Prohibition days, mostly as a strike-breaker in the garment industry where "the Brain" pioneered in labor racketeering.

The meeting took place on a Central Park bench on an autumn day in 1920. Rothstein mulled over the idea and, in short order, expanded it beyond Greenberg's dreams. Instead of buying in Canada, he decided, why not buy in England where the supply was greater?

Why not? Without hesitation Greenberg abandoned Lake Erie to the developing Purple Gang of Detroit and the Cleveland Syndicate. He turned over his trucks and warehouses in the Detroit area as collateral for a $175,000 loan from Rothstein. (Waxey Gordon cut himself in for a small piece of the action and in time that small piece would make him a major independent and blood rival of Dutch Schultz.) Eventually, the warehouses in Nassau were choked with whiskey shipped from England and waiting to be smuggled into the United States. Cases were stacked on the beaches of "Out Islands" and a wave of prosperity swept the Bahamas

Liquor smuggling from the sea grew to immense proportions. Law enforcement was far beyond the capabilities of customs and prohibition agents, so it fell upon the Coast Guard. At right, CG-128 with contraband seized in New York harbor.

At left, the *Nola,* protected by steel
armorplate, which lost a running
battle with three Coast Guard patrol
boats. Sometimes, when seizure
looked imminent, top, the crew of
the rumrunner would set the boat
afire, destroying the evidence, as
above. The courts often thwarted
the Coast Guard, too. In one court,
the story goes, a witness said he'd
found 100 cases in a seized boat.
"There is no law against carrying
cases," said the judge. "Case
dismissed."

"Big Maxey" Greenberg, Detroit bootleggger, who was bankrolled by Arnold Rothstein. Rothstein was at the peak of his career when, on November 5, 1928, he was found in the employees' entrance of the Park Central Hotel in New York with a gunshot wound in the abdomen. He died two days later.

for the first time since the defeat of the South in the Civil War ended one era of smuggling.

Meanwhile Rothstein's European agent, Harry Mather, bought 20,000 cases of Scotch in England, and found a ship to transport them. Rothstein bought a fleet of speedboats capable of carrying up to a thousand cases of whiskey. Arrangements were made to land the booze on Long Island where Rothstein had a gambling casino and friendly relations with police and the Coast Guard. All went as scheduled. Coast Guardsmen helped unload the cargo and police provided a motorcycle escort to the warehouse Rothstein had rented in Long Island City.

Eleven more crossings were made before Rothstein, recognizing that the caper was too large for one man to control, quit smuggling liquor and turned to narcotics and diamond smuggling instead. Gordon and Greenberg carried on, to be joined by scores of others such as William "Big Bill" Dwyer, Frank Costello, and Owney Madden. Rothstein used Legs Diamond to hijack the liquor cargoes others were bringing in, but he quit that too as the emerging pattern of organization became clear. As a gambler, Rothstein

Rothstein had apparently been in a card game in Room 349 (A) when he was shot. The revolver was thrown out the window and landed in the street (B). The crime was never solved. Below, his burial.

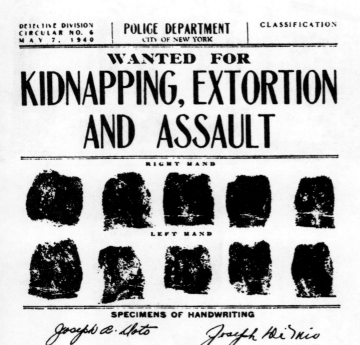

did not press his luck. Why should he—with so many avenues to profit open to a man of intelligence?

No matter how well a man figures the odds, however, there are always the random elements, the intangibles, to spoil the game. Shortly after 10 P.M. on November 4, 1928, the game was spoiled for Arnold Rothstein. He was found in the servants' entrance to the Park Central Hotel in New York, with a bullet in the stomach. Two days later he was dead. Ironically, had he lived through the day he would have won $570,000 in election bets, having put his money down on Herbert Hoover for President and Franklin D. Roosevelt for governor of New York. The murder was never solved.

In 1925, political protection on the federal level became for a time unreliable. President Harding's unexpected death on August 3, 1923, had been the prelude to scandal. Democrats sensing an issue, and paying some political debts, were busily exposing the Ohio Gang's activities. Among those talking were Jacob Stein and Gaston B. Means. Temporarily the heat was on so federal law-enforcement agencies played it safe while waiting to see if any real reforms would emerge from the sound and fury. J. Edgar Hoover was moved up from assistant director to director of the Bureau of Investigation, but the Bureau remained largely concerned with protecting administration (Republican)

interests, and under Presidents Coolidge and Hoover those interests remained the making of as many fast bucks as possible under the free-enterprise system. In view of the Teapot Dome and other scandals, however, the boys were cautioned not to be too free with their enterprise in areas of public domain.

One of those who fell victim to the confused crime and corruption climate was Frank Costello. Francesco Castiglia was his name when he was born in 1891 in the Italian village of Laropola. His father, a farmer, brought his family to New York four years later and invested in a small grocery store in New York. Conditions in the ghetto caused Costello to grumble later in life that he "was brought up like a mushroom." Quitting school at age fourteen, he sold newspapers, ran errands, organized penny-ante dice games, and finally, after three years of drifting, signed on as a deck hand on a banana boat plying the Caribbean. The tropics did not attract him, however, and in two years he returned to his aimless life in New York. Gradually, he acquired a police record, a wife, and a working relationship with such men as Joe Doto, who liked to be called Joe Adonis, or by his friends, "Joey A." Adonis headed the Broadway Mob of rumrunners. In the fall of 1925, Costello was indicted for rumrunning, but displaying the agility that was later to win him the nickname of "the Politician," he beat the rap.

Frank Costello served a jail term in 1915 for carrying a gun. He didn't like jail, and thereafter he set out to become a big shot—a white-collar criminal rather than a gun-carrying punk.

"We were just friends. I didn't know anything about his business." From left, Marjorie Marsul with Pete Licavoli, her friend; Kiki Roberts, Follies girl, "Legs" Diamond's friend; Virginia Hill, Bugsy Siegel's friend. Below, Inez Norton, Arnold Rothstein's friend; Lucky Luciano and friends at a party in Rome.

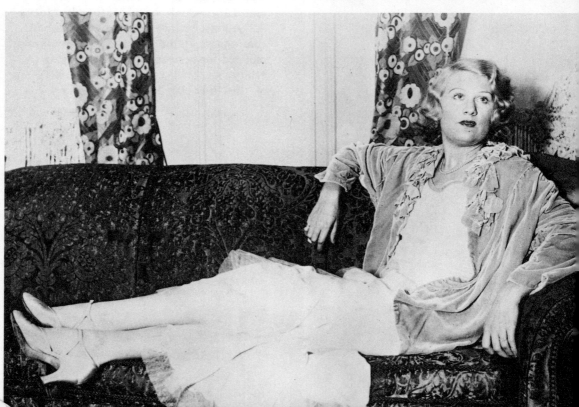

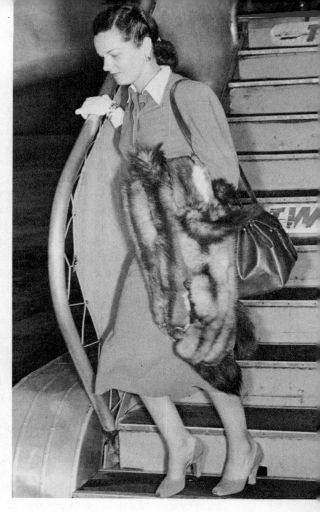

His police record never bothered him much. His wife eventually made purchases that opened the door to the Internal Revenue Service, but it was associations with such men as Adonis that made it possible for Costello to become a big shot.

Around Adonis's Broadway Mob a varied assortment of gangs and gangsters began to orbit. Most of them would eventually fall into the sun, so to speak, and so become part of a greater organization.

The Bugs and Meyer Mob was one of these. It evolved as a gun-for-hire gang, ready to supply fast cars and trucks as well as skilled drivers and expert killers to anyone willing to pay. Whether the assignment was to protect a convoy of booze or hijack it made little difference to Lansky, the executive, or Siegel, the field commander. When the Broadway Mob needed additional troops to safeguard its expanding operations, the Bugs and Meyer Mob was hired. It only took three months and two days for Adonis, Costello, and the rest to decide it was cheaper to make Lansky and Siegel partners than to pay their fees. Once inside the organization, Lansky moved rapidly to a position of co-equal. One of the things he had going for him was his friendship with Lucky Luciano.

Lucky, at this point, was a minor figure in the overall crime picture, but he was a

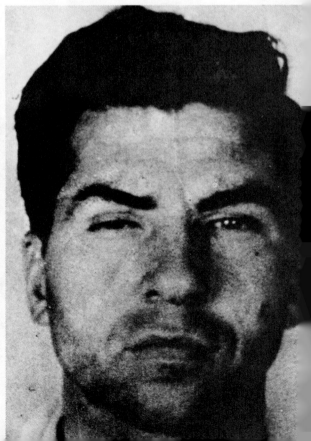

Above, Joe Adonis, born Giuseppe Doto in Italy, who obtained a birth certificate listing his birthplace as Passaic, N.J. When this was finally discovered, he was deported. "Lucky" Luciano earned his nickname by surviving hours of torture by rival gangsters.

Federal customs officers seize four
boats in the Detroit River carrying
196 cases of beer.

growing power in the Mafia. As a self-pro-claimed "Young American" he had made league with Lansky to seize power from the "Mustache Petes" of whatever ethnic background. The Mafia was in its usual state of intrigue, and Luciano, backed by the guns of the Bugs and Meyer Mob, was but waiting his chance. Yet as important as Lansky was to Lucky's plans, the relationship wasn't one-sided. The Broadway Mob wanted peace and stability, and if Lansky could win it by friendship as well as by force, so much the better.

Another contributing factor to the developing combination was the Reinfeld Syndicate. The Reinfelds came to the United States prior to 1910 and worked as bartenders and tailors until Prohibition gave them their big chance. In alliance with the Bronfman brothers of Canada, they quickly developed a fail-safe system of smuggling. It was illegal to slip liquor purchased in Canada to the United States, so it was sent to the French islands of St. Pierre and Miquelon in the St. Lawrence River. There the cargoes were "re-exported" ostensibly to all sorts of destinations but in reality to "Rum Rows" off Boston, New York, and some other East Coast cities. The French didn't care. The "Rum Rows" were located at a point just outside the United States legal jurisdiction—the distance varied from three to twelve miles. To bring liquor to that point was perfectly legal. Not until the booze was brought inside the nation's territorial waters was the Prohibition law violated. Ships anchored along Rum Row and their cargoes were legally sold to persons ashore—bootleggers—who then put their purchases onto fast speedboats and slipped into deserted beaches, inlets, or, if protection was solid enough, docks. Trucks waiting there formed convoys, well guarded against hijackers, and moved the valuable cargo to warehouses where, as demand required, it was sold to retail outlets after perhaps being "cut" several times

to increase quantity at the expense of quality.

The Broadway Mob bought a lot of the supply shipped in by the Reinfeld Syndicate, and in time the two outfits merged. A New Jersey boy, Abner "Longie" Zwillman, who began as a truckdriver, went on to achieve great power in the Reinfeld Syndicate and later in the larger organization that developed. With cooperation from Lansky, he became the major power in New Jersey after such stubborn independents as Waxey Gordon and Dutch Schultz were eliminated. But that was for the future.

In addition to buying from such wholesalers as the Reinfeld Syndicate and Bill McCoy, whose liquor became a standard for uncut excellence, the Broadway Mob brought in liquor as well. Lansky became the "traveling man" for the organization, roaming from the Bahamas to Canada and touching at such ports of entry as Miami, Savannah, Philadelphia, Boston, Cleveland, and Detroit. Still faithful to the hopes for cooperation he shared with Luciano, he kept alert for other bright young men and formed alliances which have endured over the decades: alliances with such men as Nig Rosen in Philadelphia, Joe Linsey in Boston, Moe Dalitz in Cleveland, Joe Massei in Detroit, Yiddi Bloom in Minneapolis-St. Paul. These friendships not only served Lansky personally in his bid for power, but they proved to be the skeleton of the nation-wide syndicate to come.

Everywhere the pattern was the same. Bright and hungry young men, many first-generation Americans, were turning against their elders and demanding the application of modern business methods to crime. Not all such groups were lucky. Perhaps most ironic was the fate of the Purple Gang of Detroit; its name survived decades after the original gang members had scattered.

The Purple Gang began prior to Prohibition as a group of young toughs preying on shopkeepers in the Jewish ghetto in downtown Detroit. The fact that the youths would

Abner "Longie" Zwillman, one of the few gansters to take his own life.

Detroit's Purple Gang began as strong-arm men and progressed to rumrunning. A war with a rival gang was their undoing. After two "massacres," Detroit had had enough. Here are assorted members of the Purple Gang (except for the police inspector, at left above), including Thomas "Yonnie" Licavoli, top right, one of the hoods brought in by the gang for reinforcement.

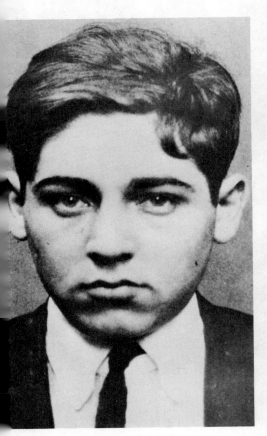
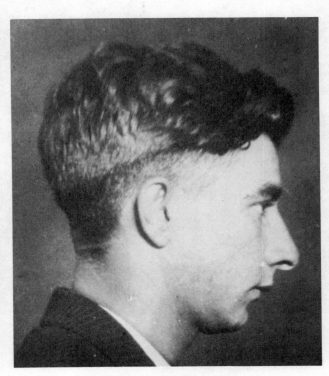

In the 1931 Collingwood Manor
Apartment massacre, three of the
Purple Gang were killed. Apparently
they had been lured there for an
amicable conference. Above, Solly
Levine, driver of their car, is
questioned. Fifteen bullets were
fired. Each man was shot in the
back. Two clutched freshly lighted
cigars in their hands; the third had
a cigar in his mouth. At right,
attorney Rodney Baxter points to
bullet holes while prosecutor Harry
Foy (with hat) looks on.

rob and harass their own people caused the
shopkeepers to consider them tainted—
purple. And the name stuck.

In the early 1920s, the gang came to
maturity as strong-arm goons in the city's
version of the industry-wide cleaners and
dyers "war" between unions and manage-
ment. They were hired to "persuade" employees of the various companies not to join
labor unions then seeking to organize the
industry. One of their employers was Moe
Dalitz who, with his brother Louis, had
opened the first of several laundries in
Detroit. Dalitz became associated on an
executive level with the Purple Gang which
soon became involved in various aspects of
the liquor business including rumrunning.

100

Unfortunately, some of the younger members of the gang were hot-tempered, and Dalitz—an "old man" in his early twenties—was unable to keep them out of trouble. Rivalry developed between the Purples and the Little Jewish Navy, another gang of rumrunners. Both sides began hiring mercenaries, mostly young Italian-Americans from other cities. The Purple Gang brought in the Licavoli boys, Thomas and Peter, from St. Louis, and a Chicago-type gang war blossomed. After the Milaflores Apartment massacre in 1926, Moe Dalitz pulled out of the Purple Gang and went to Akron, Ohio.

The Purples continued their merry and bloody way until they killed three men in the Collingwood Manor Apartment massacre. This created such heat that the gang dis-

persed. Some of its members went to prison, others left Detroit to make new lives in other cities. Even the hired troops under the Licavolis had to scatter, but eventually Peter Licavoli returned to build a new empire and the press, in Detroit and elsewhere, referred to it as the Purple Gang. The name was just too colorful to discard.

In Akron, Moe Dalitz got together with three other bootleggers—Morris Kleinman, Sam Tucker, and Louis Rothkopf—to pool resources and gain a monopoly of rumrunning across Lake Erie. Many years later, Sam Tucker in a petition filed in United States Tax Court in connection with some property acquired in 1936, gave this summary of syndicate evolution:

The four charter members of the powerful Cleveland Syndicate and one of their associates in 1951. These men joined forces during Prohibition to bring whiskey from Canada to rum rows along Lake Erie, and then went into other profitable enterprises. Above, from left, Moe Dalitz, Sam Tucker, Louis Rothkopf. Right, Morris Kleinman. Far right, associate Pete Licavoli.

"For some years prior to 1936, Messrs. Moe Dalitz, Sam Tucker, Louis Rothkopf, and Morris Kleinman were associated together in various enterprises . . . as sort of an entity in various and sundry business transactions involving laundries, real estate, night clubs, and casino operations. They have always been equal partners in these various and sundry transactions."

In the annals of organized crime, one will not find a better statement of basic relationships. That "sort of entity" was the Cleveland Syndicate and it endured through four decades of economic, political, and social change. Much of its success could be attributed to the belief of its leaders that there was, indeed, enough for everyone. Such a theory made the Cleveland bosses natural allies of Luciano and Lansky in New York, and of other young men in other cities, and contributed much to the development of a system of regional alliances that became the National Syndicate. Peter Licavoli, for instance, thanks to his old association with Dalitz, was able to become part of the

From top, Al Polizzi, another
Cleveland Syndicate associate;
Harry Stromberg, alias Nig Rosen.

general combination that developed from Detroit to Buffalo under the authority of the Cleveland Syndicate.

Dalitz and his group, realizing the necessity of a stable power base, had begun operations in Cleveland where a Mafia gang known as the Mayfield Road Mob was challenging the power of the Porello brothers, victors over the Lonardo brothers. The Mayfield Road Mob was led by Tony, Frank, and Peter Milano, and Al and Chuck Polizzi. With political protection bought by Dalitz and his associates, the Porellos were wiped out and Frank Milano became capo of Cleveland. By then, of course, it was obvious that big profits in Prohibition lay in rumrunning. By past precedent the Mayfield Road Mob should have felt obliged to wage war with the Jewish leaders of the Syndicate—but it didn't happen.

Contributing to the working arrangements that evolved between the potential rivals was Charles "Chuck" Polizzi. As the avowed cousin of "Big Al" Polizzi, Chuck had great power and influence on Mayfield Road. But, contrary to the general assumption, Chuck was not of Italian birth. His parents, who were Jewish, died when Chuck was a boy. Relatives of Big Al living in the Woodland district unofficially adopted the orphan and raised him as a member of the family. He used several names before picking Charles when he grew up, but thanks to the influence of "cousin" Al he was accepted on Mayfield Road as a Polizzi. He was also accepted by Dalitz and company, who knew of his background, and when Morris Kleinman was sent "away" briefly on an income-tax rap in 1933, Chuck Polizzi was appointed to replace him. When Kleinman got out in 1936, Chuck continued as a junior partner and had a "piece" of more Syndicate projects than anyone else with a non-Jewish name. In a real sense he served as a bridge between two cultures, permitting rival groups to work together for the benefit of both.

The citizens of Cleveland had reason to be grateful. Abruptly the gang killings, which for a time rivaled the body count of Chicago, ceased, and an honest citizen could walk safely to his favorite speakeasy. Moreover, he could buy there good Canadian whiskey instead of rot-gut from the corn-sugar stills of the Woodland district. Police and sheriffs' deputies found a steady, safe, and reliable source of extra cash, and politicians found new financial patrons. Even Eliot Ness, that old "untouchable" from Chicago, served a spell as Cleveland safety director before settling down to private employment as a consultant with a list of interesting clients. Alas, he died before he became a television legend in the 1950s.

In May, 1929, the first major gangland convention met at the Hotel President in Atlantic City, New Jersey. Al Capone attended from Chicago and enjoyed an emotional reunion with Johnny Torrio, back from his travels and deeply involved in New York rackets. Observers were there from as far away as Kansas City, but the principal business concerned the leaders of East Coast gangs. Torrio, who had found a willing ally in Lansky, advocated the same kind of working alliance that he had tried in Chicago. It was finally agreed to and became known to history as the "Big Seven" although more than a dozen top figures were represented. Charles "King" Solomon was represented from Boston; Nig Rosen from Philadelphia; Longie Zwillman from New Jersey. Torrio brought in Daniel Walsh of Providence, Rhode Island, Frank Zagarino, with whom he was in partnership, and Dutch Schultz whom he was financing in the numbers racket and the essential subsidiary, the bonding business. The Broadway Mob, the single largest outfit, was well represented by Lansky, Adonis, Costello, and a little man who was rapidly becoming dreaded as Louis "Lepke" Buchalter.

Agreement was reached which fixed prices

From top, Louis "Lepke" Buchalter; Charles "King" Solomon with Dorothy England.

of booze along the East Coast. Quotas were established so no one could bring in more than he needed and undersell his competitors. Arrangements were made to pool the supply in case shortages developed in any area. A central clearing house was established in New York City where all purchases and deliveries were recorded and payments made.

The arrangement did not go as far as Torrio and Lansky hoped, but it still represented a tremendous step toward eventual consolidation. To Mafia observers, that gangsters operating outside the law could make such complex and far-reaching deals and, moreover, get compliance from independent and greedy men scattered over a thousand miles of coast was something of a miracle. Luciano angrily determined to end the civil war in the Honored Society that prevented it from taking part in the big chance.

The revolt against the new capo di capi re, Joe "the Boss" Masseria, actually began with the murder of Gaspare Milazzo, capo of Detroit and a native of the Sicilian town of Castellammare del Golfo. Salvatore Maranzano, also a native of that town, appealed to all his former townsmen to avenge the murder. He gathered around him a group of *fuoriusciti* (outlaws) and declared war. Masseria responded by securing a sentence of death against all natives of Castellammare del Golfo. As Maranzano's power grew, men from Palermo whose former leader had been the late capo di capi re, Toto D'Aquila, and who resented their fall from power, joined forces with him and the vendetta took on the aspects of a holy war. As Nicola Gentile, an eyewitness to the events, described it:

"A lot of youths desiring to avenge their friends put themselves at the disposition of Maranzano. The group began to enlarge. The outlaws, so called, began to meet on the farms of friends, taking possession of them. From the farms they initiated their purging

operations, eliminating those that Maranzano disliked and inviting others to pass to his side. With this system Maranzano succeeded in penetrating a lot of cities of the United States, planting terror everywhere. Other youths passed to his side and others contributed large sums."

Gentile, as a well-known and popular figure, saw an opportunity to create a third force and take command of the Honored Society when its members tired of bloodshed. He suspected that Lucky Luciano was planning to do the same thing, but the possibility didn't alarm him. Unaware of Lucky's secret alliance with Lansky, Gentile considered him a mere young upstart with no prestige outside New York.

The revolt was different from other battles within the Mafia only in its size. In the past, national leaders had been upset by sudden coups usually delivered by persons trusted by the victim. Maranzano tried no coup, relying instead on a war of attrition. He continued to gain ground as more and more Masseria men defected. Gentile and his friends decided the time had come to force a solution. They arranged for a general assembly of the Mafia in Boston. It was understood that neither Masseria nor Maranzano would attend. A special commission was appointed by the assembly to seek a meeting with Maranzano and offer enough concessions to end the war. The commission met in New York at the Pennsylvania Hotel but Maranzano did not show up.

Now for the first time the Mafia began to feel heat from public opinion in New York. According to Gentile, "Once in a while a fratello would be killed and with him some innocent citizen. The papers of New York started to get in an uproar, asking the responsible organs of government to put an end to this gangster war that was costing honest citizens their lives." The chief of police called Masseria in and told him "in

his boys led by Vito Genovese, his chief lieutenant, shot Joe the Boss six times in the back and head. It was April 15, 1931.

Gentile, who hoped to use Luciano for his own purposes, quickly went to Lucky's apartment. Vincent Troia, a friend of Maranzano, was called in by Luciano.

"Don Vicenzo," he said, "tell your *compare* Maranzano that we have killed Masseria—not to serve him but for our own personal reasons. Tell him that if he should touch even the hair of even a personal enemy of ours we will wage war to the end. Tell him that within twenty-four hours he must give us an affirmative answer for a meeting at a locality which we will pick out . . ."

So spoke the "Combination" through the mouth of Lucky Luciano, leaving no doubt that in this time of transition a new force had emerged with which Maranzano would have to deal. And Maranzano, while not willing to forget his ambitions, was quick to accept the new realities.

The meeting took place next day. A new general assembly was called for Chicago with Capone—who was a second cousin to Luciano—agreeing to pay the bills. Gentile made a last effort there to replace the capo di capi re system with a commission, but Maranzano, now very much the hero, defeated the move and not even the silver tongue of Gentile could prevent the election of the ex-outlaw as the new boss of all the bosses. Luciano made no move to interfere, not wanting to polarize the Mafia once more until the members had a chance to evaluate their new leader. He was confident that Maranzano would follow the bloody tradition of the Honored Society, so a waiting game was indicated. He was right.

The new capo di capi re established himself in a luxurious apartment behind the Hotel Commodore. It flanked Grand Central, a busy place full of people and police. In such a location, Maranzano reasoned, it would be difficult to kill him. A study was converted into a guardroom and two teams, each working a twelve-hour shift, were installed there. He traveled in an armored car to another fortress at 230 Park Avenue where his offices were located. Although the money flowed in from capos anxious to cur , favor, Maranzano drew up a "death list" of sixty names. On the list were Luciano, Adonis, Genovese, and almost all capos of importance.

In the moment of crisis, Luciano unveiled his secret weapon, the Bugs and Meyer Mob. With no member of the Mafia could he feel safe. Lansky and Siegel guarded Lucky day and night, until, agreeing that the moment had come, they went on the offensive.

Six experienced killers accompanied by one Italian who could identify Maranzano went to the office of the Eagle Building Corporation, 230 Park Avenue, and knocked on the door. They identified themselves as federal agents and were admitted. Drawing pistols, they forced Maranzano's bodyguards to put their faces and hands against the wall. Gentile has told what happened next:

"While the Jews with leveled pistols held the followers of Maranzano motionless, one of the Jews went into the corridor and called the Italian, asking him which of these men was Maranzano."

Maranzano recognized the Italian, and being under the illusion the whole affair was a raid by Prohibition agents, he said:

" 'Peppino, you know that I am Maranzano and that I am responsible for the office. They can make any search they want here because there is no contraband here. This office is commercial.' "

Gentile's account continued: "No sooner were the Jews certain that Maranzano was actually in their hands than they led him to his [private] office and in order to avoid noise tried to strangle him. Thereafter they tried to finish him off by stabbing him, but the doomed man by virtue of his desperation got loose, and because he was possessed by a certain strength augmented by fear, he sought to fight. The others emptied their

110

pistols into him, killing him instantly."

It was September 10, 1931. Maranzano had ruled for five days less than five months. His body bore four gunshot wounds and five stab wounds. When the Bugs and Meyer Mob bumped somebody they bumped him good.

But the killing had just begun. Luciano's men were waiting on the street. When told the mission was successful they scattered to telephones "and informed the boys in various parts of New York, advising them that they could start the purging operation." The "slaughter of the Sicilian Vespers" began.

The slaughter wasn't confined to New York. Across the country next day the "young Americans" of the Mafia, aided and abetted by the young Americans of the local combination where needed, executed the "Mustache Petes" of the Mafia, according to a well conceived plan. Since no local law enforcement had facilities for keeping tabs on killings outside its jurisdiction, and since the Bureau of Investigation didn't believe there was such a thing as the Mafia, no official body count was available until 1970 when former Attorney General Ramsey Clark placed the total at forty. The source of his information isn't mentioned.

The Mafia was "Americanized," and it took a back seat thereafter in the council rooms of the multi-ethnic "Combination." Another general assembly was called for Chicago and this time, guided by Luciano, the members, "tired and enlightened by experience," abolished the capo di capi re system and vested national authority in a commission. According to Gentile, who was there, the commission included:

Luciano, capo of the family formerly bossed by Masseria; Vincent Mangano, capo of D'Aquila's former family; Joe Profaci, capo of a Brooklyn family; Peppino (Joe Bananas) Bonnano, capo of a New York family; Capone, boss of part of Chicago and even then awaiting trial in federal

230 Park Avenue in New York, site of a Mafia execution in 1931.

court; Gaetano Gagliano, capo of a New York family formerly headed by Gaetano Reina; and Frank Milano, capo of Cleveland and ally of the Cleveland Syndicate.

Gentile was not rewarded for his long years of service, a fact he loudly deplored. It was Luciano who, as first among equals on the commission, would be the real boss. But Luciano's power depended largely on his relationship with Lansky and others of the "Big Seven." The "Americanization" of the Mafia was important to the future plans of such men as Lansky and Torrio because it assured an end to civil wars that interfered with business and caused "heat" from public officials. Luciano knew his role in the Mafia would automatically give him a place on the board of directors of any larger organization, and with that he was content. The Mafia remained what it had been—a society, a brotherhood, consisting of autonomous "families" in scattered cities, connected only by tradition and blood lines. Some capos in the decades to come achieved great wealth and standing in their own areas, but none became national figures by virtue of their membership in the Honored Society. Men like Luciano, Adonis, and Costello did achieve great recognition, but chiefly because of their association with the National Crime Syndicate.

It should be noted that five of the seven members of the commission were from the New York area where, of course, Luciano was strong. This not only indicates Lucky's concern for his personal position, but illustrates how unimportant he considered the rest of the country. Of the two "outsiders" chosen to represent the "boondocks," Capone was related to Luciano and within days after his election to the commission he was sentenced to eight years in prison. The Chicago Syndicate would remain powerful, but the Mafia in the Windy City faded into the background. Milano of Cleveland was, in a real sense, a creature of Moe Dalitz and

his partners, and that "sort of entity" was closely allied with Lansky. Milano eventually retired to an estate in Mexico near Veracruz, and his successor, "Big Al" Polizzi, moved to Miami where, years later, he became a business associate of Charles "Bebe" Rebozo, the political confidant of President Richard M. Nixon. John Scalish, who for years worked in Cleveland Syndicate casinos as a clerk, eventually became capo of Cleveland—and no one cared.

Nicola Gentile tried to make himself useful to the new order, but was blocked from positions of profit as well as honor. The new generation had no use for his talents as a peace maker. Later he was to write:

"These men had forgotten me whom they had used to resolve many risky situations. Meanwhile, the fruits of my labors had been harvested by these 'papaveri' who continued to use me—pushing me around from one point in the United States to another. O ingratitude of humanity!"

Eventually, Gentile would be forced into the narcotics racket—the most dangerous and degrading of all those organized by Arnold "the Brain" Rothstein. In 1937 he was caught in New Orleans—his pride made him insist he was framed—and released on bond. Under orders from his bosses, for Nicola had sunk low, he jumped bond and sneaked back to Sicily, where he brooded over the wrongs done to him and devised elaborate schemes to force the Mafia to compensate him for services rendered. More than two decades later, one such scheme backfired and brought the all but forgotten Gentile to the attention of federal officials. In an entirely unexpected way, Nicola got his revenge.

Meanwhile, economic and political events conspired to realize the dream of Lansky, Torrio, Lepke and—yes, Luciano, as in 1934 at a New York hotel the National Crime Syndicate was created. Out of many elements dropped into the melting pot, a single entity emerged.

4 THE BIG HEAT

On November 29, 1971, Martin Loewy, acting chief of the organized crime section of the Justice Department, admitted the relationship of crime to the economy. He was quoted as saying:

"Organized crime is not ordinarily short of cash. When business is slow it leaves room for organized crime to take over. What starts out as a creditor ends up as a partner."

Loewy's observations, while directed at current conditions, apply with special validity to the situation existing in the country after October 29, 1929—Black Tuesday. On that day there was panic on Wall Street and an era that began with Harding and "normalcy" and continued through "Hoover prosperity" came to an abrupt and shocking end.

In the months and years that followed, the Great Depression deepened across the land: unemployment, bankruptcy, grim want. Steadily conditions grew worse, the climax coming early in 1933 when those banks that had survived now locked their doors. The only people left with money, so went the bitter joke, were the bootleggers.

This was the most important moment in the history of organized crime, and one completely overlooked by law-enforcement officials until Loewy's comment in 1971. For the bootleggers did have cash, millions times millions of dollars, and it was stashed away in shoeboxes hidden under beds, in wall safes in clothes closets, in cans buried in back yards. It was, in other words, liquid.

Being rich prior to Black Tuesday was, of course, important to the men struggling to put the business of crime on an organized basis, but it wasn't vital so long as a lot of legitimate people were also wealthy. But to have cash when no one else had it, when the bankers and the brokers and the business tycoons were jumping out of office windows or, more privately, blowing out their brains, ah, that was the edge.

For in the three years after the crash, until Franklin D. Roosevelt persuaded the country that the only thing it had to fear was fear itself, those businessmen who didn't kill themselves turned by the thousands to the only men with money and credit—the gangsters. They came hat in hand, and they went away with operating capital and

The   Sun

Copyright, 1929, by The Sun Printing and Publishing Association

6   NEW YORK, FRIDAY, OCTOBER 25, 1929.

NKER DIES.

Laimbeer.

X-BANKER SUDDENLY

Laimbeer Dies t Attack.

Laimbeer, formerly and head of the ent of the National uddenly at 9:55 A ome, 450 East Fifty- Death was due to tion.

widow of a partner bishop, Laimbeer & st woman to gain e field of finance. t of an association organized in 1923. of the women's de- National City, with stant cashier, in headquarters being ranch at Madison -second street.

had headed the ent of the United Trust Company, arious branches in hich women's ac- ted. She resigned City Bank on Oc- reason not being

had suffered from r some time, but not regarded as death came to er physician Dr her bedside. Pres- trie Laimbeer.

Mrs. Laimbeer's ..

TRADER IS MISSING AFTER STOCK CRASH

Last Seen Tearing Up Ticker Tape in Wall Street.

Bernard H. Sandler, a lawyer, of 225 Broadway, received a call today from Mrs. Abraham Germansky, of the Hotel Beacon, who said her husband had been absent from home since yesterday morning. Germansky, said to be a real estate operator and a millionaire, was, according to Mr. Sandler, a heavy investor in securi- ties on the Stock Exchange.

According to the story told by Mrs. Germansky to Mr. Sandler he was seen late yesterday by a friend on Wall street, near the Exchange, with a strip of ticker tape in his hand. According to Mrs. German- sky her informant said he was tear- ing the tape into bits and scattering it on the sidewalk as he walked to- ward Broadway.

Germansky is about 50 years old and has two children.

WITNESSES LIST $93,000 SENT TO WARDER'S HOME

Dell' Osso Avers He Carried $73,000 From Ferrari to State Official.

LABATE SAYS HE TOOK $20,000

State Superintendent of Banks, from Francesco M. Ferrari, late president of the looted City Trust Company, and of additional amounts similarly carried in sealed envelopes was re- cited today by Gennaro Dell' Osso.

Continued on Twenty-fourth Page.

Babson Sees Orderly Decline

Predicts It Will Follow Rally in Stocks and Be Succeeded by Dullness

Roger W. Babson, the statistician, said today in a state- ment exclusive to The Sun:
"The market should rally from the present figures due to

EXTRA

HOOVER FINDS COUNTRY ON A VERY SOUND BASIS

WASHINGTON, Oct. 25 (A. P.).— President Hoover said today the funda- mental structure of the country is on a very sound basis.

Heads of Bankrupt Firm Sentenced to Prison

NEW HAVEN, Oct. 25 (U. P.).— The three partners of the bankrupt $5,000,000 Parker-Smith Mortgage Investment Company were sentenced to State's prison by Superior Court Judge Isaac Wolfe here today.

The defendants, John E. Parker, the president; Clarence V. Smith, secretary, and Paul M. Smith, treas- urer, were found guilty by a jury yesterday on thirty-one counts of embezzlement.

Parker received three to six years in State's prison on the eleventh count and one year each on the other thirty counts, the sentences to run concurrently. The Smiths received terms of five to eight years on the eleventh count, with one year sen- tences on each of the other counts, the sentences to run concurrently.

Husband Out of Work, Wife Commits Suicide

After two hours of work with an inhalator a gas company emergency squad today was unable to bring back to life Mrs. Elsie Thripp, 30 years old, whose body had been dis- covered in the kitchen of her home, 24 Congress street, New Dorp, Staten Island.

Wesley Thripp, the husband, ar- rived home and found the door locked. He forced an entrance and found his wife seated on a chair be- fore the gas range, with three jets opened. He told the police his wife had been worried because he was un- able to find work.

GAINS SHOWN AT CLOSE O

Closing Bid and As

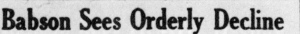

partners. This is the period when organized crime infiltrated big business, especially those industries having a cash flow like the movies or those catering to basic human needs like restaurants, clothing manufacturers, grocery stores. Moreover, by getting in on the ground floor, they grew with the companies. The liquor industry was one excellent vehicle. With repeal in 1933, new legitimate companies were formed. In the board rooms of many of them were such men as Torrio, Lansky, and Costello.

On the political level there was also significant change, and for the same reason —money, or the lack of it. In the past, politicians had turned to businessmen for necessary campaign contributions. The gangster had been at the mercy, more or less, of the elected official. Indeed, many city gangs in pre-Prohibition days had been used as instruments for political party discipline. But, abruptly, it was the gangster in the driver's seat. He gave the orders to the politician. Moreover, as time went by, he dictated to the party as to which candidate was to get the nomination. The candidates now solicited the support of gangsters, and, after election, earned their continued support by deeds not words.

The reversal of tradition was well illustrated at the Democratic national convention in Chicago in 1932. Almost everyone assumed the man nominated would be the next President. The battle was between Roosevelt and that "happy warrior," Al Smith, the 1928 nominee. The New York delegation was split. Tammany Hall's Albert C. Marinelli led one group pledged to Smith, and West Side boss Jimmy Hines led another eager to fight for Roosevelt. Nothing unusual about that. But accompanying Marinelli was Lucky Luciano, and sharing Hines's quarters was Frank Costello. Regardless of who won, the boys would have friends in camp.

After his victory in Chicago and later in the general election, Roosevelt set out

President Hoover was not a good prophet, as the "Extra" shows. Above, a self-explanatory bumper plate.

OUR NEXT
FRANKLIN D.
KANSAS
GEORGIA
HIS
SOUTHERN HOME
FOR
PRESIDENT
DELAWARE
FOR
PRESIDENT

deliberately to destroy the power of the big-city bosses. By centralizing welfare programs in Washington, he removed much of the popular support for the old-fashioned boss who could be counted on to lend money in time of need and supply a ton of coal during a cold winter. Moreover, under Roosevelt's leadership the Intelligence Unit of the Bureau of Internal Revenue was assigned specifically to break up the big-city gangs. Huey Long in Louisiana was one major target since Long for a time threatened to develop into a popular rival of Roosevelt. Nucky Johnson, host for the 1929 gangland convention at Atlantic City, was another target. The Pendergast machine in Kansas City came under attack as well.

All these factors, while designed for other purposes, helped strengthen the national power of the Mob. As the old order collapsed, the hoods moved in and set up invisible governments just beneath the surface. The extent of the takeover varied from city to city and state to state, but the unholy alliance of crime, business, and politics prospered well beyond the average citizen's conception. One thing remained the same, however— the goal of making fast bucks as quickly as possible.

In this time of transition, the end of Prohibition was another important change. Many of the brighter intellects had recognized that the liquid gold could not flow forever and had prepared for the inevitable. While J. Edgar Hoover warned that

ST. LOUIS POST-DISPATCH

Sunday Post-Dispatch 68 Pages T

Section   Pages   Section
First (News) .... 12 Sixth (Editorial, Pho
Second (Sports) ...... and Drama
Third (Society) .... Rotogravure
Fourth (Real Estate) .. 13 Magazine
Fifth (Wants) .... Comics

For Auto News, See Page 3, Part 4
For Radio News, See Page 3, Part 4

VOL. 85. No. 181.   **PART ONE**   ST. LOUIS, SUNDAY MORNING, MARCH 5, 1933.   PAGES 1—12A   ★★★★★   PRICE **10** CE

BANK HOLIDAY NATION - WIDE; ACTION BY U.S. IS AWAITED

Gov. Lehman Indicates He Will Not Proceed With Plans Until Federal Program Is Announced — New York Clearing House to Issue Certificates.

DELAWARE LAST STATE AFFECTED

Unprecedented Withdraw—

TWO-DAY MISSOURI BANKING HOLIDAY MAY BE EXTENDED UNTIL NEXT FRIDAY

Gov. Park and Legislators Working on Problem of Allowing Depositories to Reopen Without Undergoing a Flood of Withdrawals.

EMERGENCY BILLS STARTED IN SENATE

Would Give Gover—

ROOSEVELT IN OFFICE SAYS HE WILL CALL ON CONGRESS FOR "WAR TIME POWERS" IF EMERGENCY REQUIRE

Chief Justice Hughes Administering the Oath to President Roosevelt

HUGE CROW HEARS H DEDICA SELF TO I

Roosevelt is elected and the "real beer" trucks roll once again.

kidnapping would be the new "in" racket, men like Lansky turned to gambling. As a social vice similar to liquor drinking, it offered a continuing market and no real public opposition despite lip service to existing laws. Sex and gambling would remain staples, Lansky believed, and in Cleveland his friends agreed. The Cleveland Syndicate began the transition to gambling casinos even as it joined with Lansky in the final and fourth stage of Prohibition.

With existing stocks exhausted, with taxes promising to make legal liquor too expensive for a country suffering from an economic depression, it was obvious that a market for a cheap but good liquor would remain even after repeal. The new liquor companies, many of them Mob-controlled, would need plenty of booze and would not inquire too closely as to the source.

Molaska Corporation officially came into existence on November 25, 1933, just ten days before liquor again became legal. The president, John Drew, was in reality, Jacob Stein, the man who had conspired with Gaston B. Means in the easy days of the Harding administration. Other officers with one exception were later identified as nominees for members of the Cleveland Syndicate: Dalitz, Tucker, and Chuck Polizzi. The exception was Moses Citron of New York, the assistant treasurer of the corporation. He proved to be the father-in-law of Meyer Lansky.

That was the official record. Long investigations later disclosed that other top names of East Coast as well as Midwest mobs were also involved: Peter Licavoli, Big Al Polizzi, Joe Adonis, Longie Zwillman, and the like. In effect, the Molaska Corporation served as a pilot vehicle for the National Crime Syndicate, the final experiment in interregional cooperation.

The purpose of Molaska was to build and operate large illicit distilleries, the largest ever discovered in the United States. The major

On April 7, 1933, thousands of speakeasies flung open their doors and became legal saloons. Here everyone is smiling at the bar of the Greenwich Village Inn in New York.

120

Molaska Corporation, created by the New York and Cleveland Syndicates, produced illicit liquor after Prohibition ended. Its still at Zanesville, Ohio, was the world's largest. In the control room, above, can be seen the seat for the master distiller. Right, the entrance to an escape tunnel. Above right, the still columns.

one was eventually found in Zanesville, Ohio. Another, almost as large, was raided at Elizabeth, New Jersey. How many operated undetected only the leaders of the Syndicate know. Some, in fact, may be operating today. Millions of gallons of good booze were manufactured and bottled. As untaxed whiskey it could be sold at half the legal price. Large as were the distilleries, they couldn't keep up with the demand. The Zanesville distillery contained mash vats requiring 48,600 pounds of sugar and 15,200 pounds of "Molaska" to fill. "Molaska" was the trade name of dehydrated molasses, a sugar substitute, which the Molaska Corporation was allegedly organized to manufacture. From these ingredients, 36,506 gallons of mash per day was produced. Thanks to continuous-process procedures, it was possible to manufacture 5,000 gallons of 190-proof alcohol every twenty-four hours. The alcohol sold for $2 per gallon wholesale, and for as much as $2.50 a quart retail. Cost, including protection, labor, fuel, and raw materials, was estimated at fifty cents per gallon.

The distillery, completely underground, featured a tunnel running to the basement of

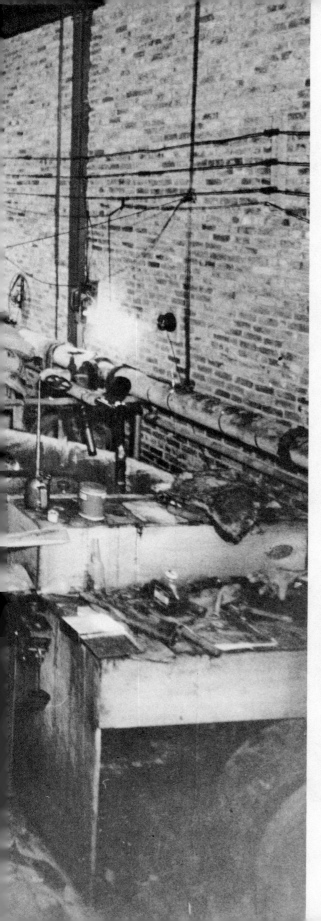

a nearby house occupied by a woman "for the sole purpose of insuring the use of the escape tunnel in case of necessity." There was equipment sufficient to manufacture 35,506 gallons of beer daily. It, like the alcohol, was shipped out in boxcar lots from a nearby railroad siding. Total cost of the plant was "at least $250,000," and it was but one of many.

Ironically illustrating the problems of disorganized law enforcement when confronted with syndicated crime, at the very time one Treasury agency was trying to prove the Zanesville distillery was owned by the Cleveland Syndicate, another agency was debating with Syndicate members over the amount of tax loss they could claim as a result of the raid. The businessmen of crime knew all the angles. They employed the best attorneys and accountants money could buy.

Liquor, both legal and illegal, has continued to be an important source of Mob income, but Molaska as a joint venture proved that a national organization was not only possible but, from a point of view of pooling resources, profitable. As gambling centers developed across the country, the name of the game was "joint venture," within the overall system.

Perhaps no better illustration of the wisdom of combining forces was the example of independents Waxey Gordon and Dutch Schultz, from whose rivalry only the Intelligence Unit of the Internal Revenue Service profited. Gordon, a veteran gangster who had operated bucket shops for Arnold Rothstein before Prohibition in the days when Rothstein was promoting stocks, had become wealthy as a pioneer rumrunner. When competition became strong, however, he switched to beer and established himself in New Jersey.

Schultz, one of the few early gangleaders who could boast of being native born, came from New York. His mother, Emma Flegenheimer, a pious and idealistic woman,

The storage room and mixing vat at the Zanesville distillery.

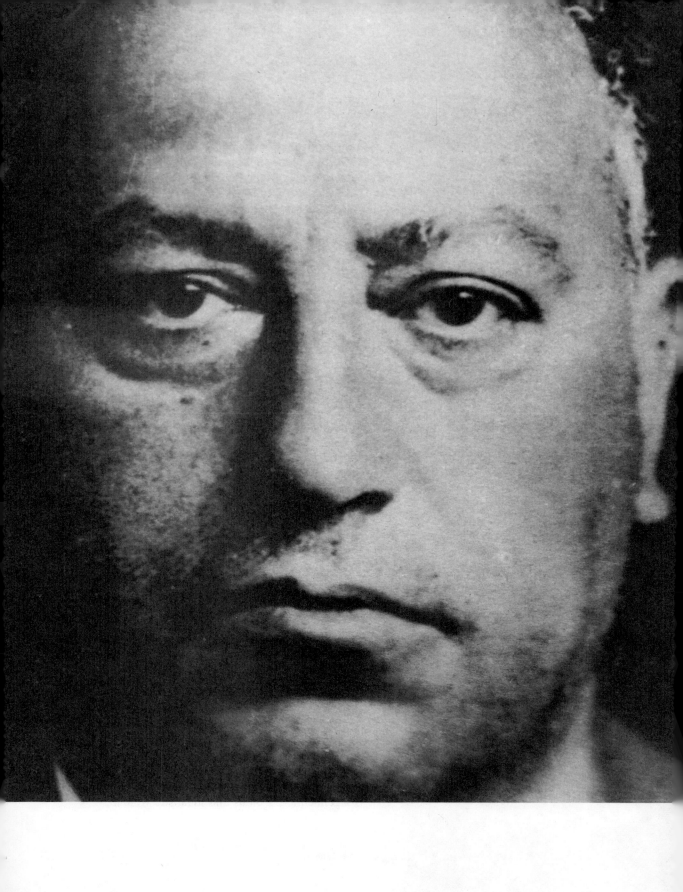

named him Arthur and dreamed of Camelot. But Public School 12 on Frisby Street was no training ground for future kings, and the boy became a member of a street gang, the "Bergens." It wasn't until he proved himself by a series of stickups and a fifteen-month stretch that the Bergens dubbed him "Dutch Schultz" after a legendary figure who had gained fame as the meanest fighter in the Bronx. With Prohibition, Dutch recruited an army of punks and formed his own liquor empire. He then branched out into race tracks, the numbers racket, the restaurant business, and others, before deciding that Gordon's beer empire was easy picking. Soon Gordon and Schultz were shooting it out, oblivious to the developing syndicate. Each man hoped, of course, to have a legal monopoly with the end of Prohibition.

Less than two weeks after beer became legal, Gordon escaped out the window of the Carteret Hotel in Elizabeth, New Jersey, as a crew of Schultz killers came in the door. Two of his men, Maxey Greenberg and Max Hassell, asleep in the next room, were murdered. Gordon went into hiding. Ten days later, on April 23, 1933, he was indicted on four counts of tax evasion. At a time when his annual income was in excess of $2 million, he had reported only $8,125. Special agents disclosed that he paid $6,000 a year in rent and the apartment contained a library with $3,800 worth of books, none of which, it seemed, had ever been opened.

Gordon was found and convicted. Sentenced to ten years, he was paroled in time to be sent back to prison for black-market activities during the Second World

Irving Wexler, alias Waxey Gordon, started as a sneak thief. His nickname came from the waxlike smoothness of his fingers, helpful for picking pockets. In the late 1920s and early 1930s he owned several hotels in midtown Manhattan, a luxurious summer home in New Jersey, several expensive automobiles, and a wardrobe that cost thousands. The authorities were never able to do anything about his more serious crimes but finally got him for tax evasion.

War. Schultz was not so lucky. He surrendered and eventually won an acquittal, but while the IRS was again preparing to indict him, he became the first victim of the newly formed Murder, Inc. It did not pay to be an obstacle to unity.

It was in the early spring of 1934, when the event much talked about by such "idealists" as Lansky and Torrio took place. At a New York hotel—said to have been the Waldorf Astoria—the National Crime Syndicate was organized. It wasn't called that, of course. Plain, simple "Syndicate" or "outfit" satisfied the non-Mafia members, and "Combineesh" was the term favored by the Honored Society.

Torrio, the man who had executive experience in both New York and Chicago, presided during most of the sessions, but Lansky, the "traveling man" for the Broadway Mob, was active behind the scenes. From Cleveland came his friend Moe Dalitz. Isadore Blumenfeld, the infamous "Kid Cann," brother of Yiddi Bloom, arrived from Minneapolis-St. Paul. Philip "Dandy Phil" Kastel, who began as a bucket-shop operator for Arnold Rothstein and was now the boss-designate of New Orleans, was present. Hyman Abrams, a close friend of Lansky who had replaced "King" Solomon in Boston when the King showed signs of ambition, brought in a delegation. Harry "Nig Rosen" Stromberg, Lansky's representative in Philadelphia, came up for the meeting. New Jersey had Longie Zwillman as its delegate. Paul "the Waiter" Ricca, considered by Lansky to be the real brains of the Chicago Syndicate, attended as an observer. Chicago, in the view of Torrio, was still too uncivilized to take part in a national association, but perhaps in time it could be educated.

The Mafia was, of course, well represented by Luciano, Adonis, Costello, and Vito Genovese, but they attended more as partners in the New York "combination" than as leaders of a separate entity. Had Luciano desired to assert the power of the Honored Society in an attempt to dominate the meeting, he would have failed. As such men as Albert Anastasia and Anthony "Little Augie" Carfano were to learn later, Lansky's power lay as much outside New York as inside, and his allies in the boondocks possessed far greater wealth and firepower than did the smart boys of the Big Town.

Reports of what happened at the sessions are somewhat vague. The New York police informants who talked were in somewhat the same boat as Joe Valachi in 1963. The celebrated songbird, when asked about conditions in Des Moines, Iowa, admitted he had never heard of the place. Similarly, the informants in 1934 got lost as soon as the discussion moved away from Brooklyn and Jersey City. Gangsters who talked many years later were also handicapped by memories blurred by time and subsequent events. Nevertheless, the basic themes of the sales pitch given the delegates is known.

Luciano told how the Mafia had been "Americanized" and promised that it would be a constructive force in the future. Anyone having a beef about a local capo could file a complaint with the "Grand Council"—the commission had become glorified—and justice would be done. By all accounts, Lucky was given a standing ovation.

Adonis described the evolution of the Big Seven, with due credit to Torrio, and Dalitz gave a bow to Lansky in explaining the operation of Molaska. Zwillman described the bloody and, from his point of view, unnecessary war in New Jersey between Gordon and Schultz. To illustrate the necessity of controlling crime, he discussed the as yet unsolved kidnapping of Charles A. Lindbergh, Jr. That it was the act of an amateur, he said, was certain, but it had created so much heat he had been forced to offer a reward for the kidnapper. Capone and some imprisoned members of the Purple

128

Moe Dalitz, who had superb organizational ability and the "big fix" in a dozen city halls.

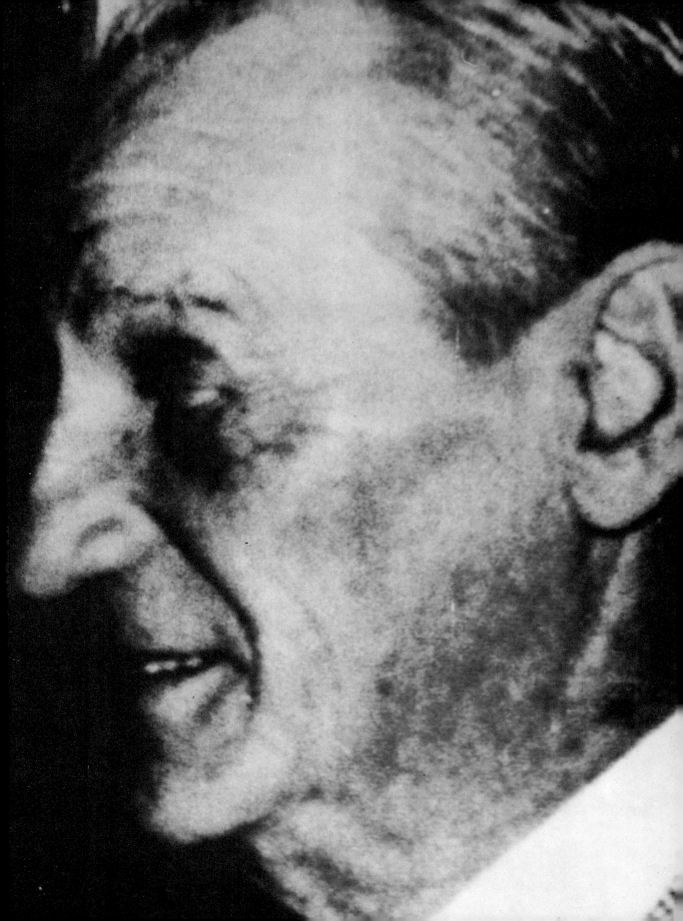

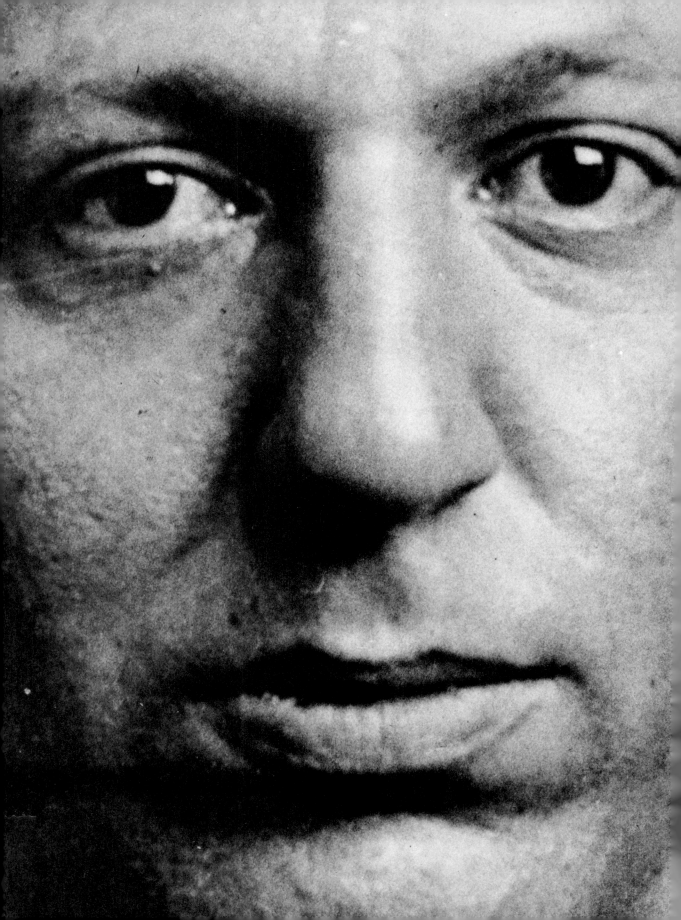

Gang didn't help matters any, he added, by offering to solve the case if released.

Other speakers outlined the proposed organization, and drew upon New Deal terminology to explain it. The national syndicate would be structured along the lines of the NRA—the National Recovery Act. There would be regional boards to control all activities, and an overall body to hear appeals. Territorial lines would be set and would be respected. Within the larger cities there would also be divisions along individual racket lines: prostitution, gambling, shylocking, protection, narcotics, extortion, and the like. Joint ventures would be encouraged in the development of new territories and certain areas such as Miami would be classed as "open" to all.

Such a massive organization could not be bossed by one individual, despite the local autonomy granted to regional groups. There would be no boss of all the bosses. Rather, there would be equality on the top level, with regional and racket chiefs sitting together as an appeals board and policy council. How would the board enforce its decisions? It was Louis Buchalter who gave the word on that subject.

Buchalter, known simply as Lepke, was a short man. He had soft eyes, a dimple in his left cheek, and a mild manner that fooled only his respectable parents. Born in 1897, he grew up in New York. He had two terms in Sing Sing Prison behind him by 1922 when he made connections with a group of professional strikebreakers. This led Lepke into labor racketeering and ultimately permitted him to gain virtual control of New York's garment district and baking industry. Along the way, Lepke became allies with Lansky who, in turn, had a good relationship with Luciano. Individually, each man was powerful, but, combined, the "Three L's" could dictate to New York.

Lepke proposed the creation of a special squad patterned after the old Bugs and Meyer Mob. It would work on demand, be

Lepke of Murder, Inc., fame.

Arthur Flegenheimer (in dark suit), better known as Dutch Schultz, beer baron of the Bronx and boss of the numbers racket in New York, with his attorney, J. Richard "Dixie" Davis. Dutch invested heavily in the nightclub business and owned the plush Embassy Club, which catered to the Park Avenue trade. He once said he should have stuck to his original name: it was too long for the headlines, and no one would have heard of him.

on call. Local bosses who needed someone killed would let a contract for that killing, and it would be done by experts. This would ensure an efficient job and at the same time eliminate the danger and expense of maintaining individual execution squads. No one, moreover, whatever his beef, would be permitted to kill outside his territory. If he had a justified complaint grave enough to require death, the sentence would be passed by the ruling commission.

The delegates liked the idea, and Lepke was authorized to create the group later to be famous as Murder, Inc.

Everything went very smoothly, indicating perhaps the power of an idea whose time had come. Special committees were set up to agree on technical details. There were few disputes even on the allocation of territories. Ratification of the existing realities was the order of the day. Thus five years later, Dixie Davis, attorney for Dutch Schultz, was to write:

"Moey Davis [in New York Dalitz was known as Davis] became the power in Cleveland, and anyone who questioned it would have to deal with Lucky and Meyer and the Bug [Siegel]."

Dixie Davis was one of the few eyewitnesses to the creation of the syndicate to talk. Unlike such later celebrated songbirds as Joseph Valachi, Davis's testimony actually helped convict important people, but historians of crime soon forgot him. That is unfortunate, for Davis was an interesting person in his own right and a forerunner of a new breed of syndicate attorneys to come.

Born in New York City in 1904, he graduated from Syracuse University and the Columbia Law School as J. Richard Davis, but was nicknamed "Dixie" because of the soft speech and relaxed manner he cultivated. He began offering to defend numbers-racket defendants, petty punks all, at cut-rate prices, and soon became acquainted with the big boss, Dutch Schultz. Behind Schultz was John Torrio, of course, and the team seemed

From left, J. Edgar Hoover; William Stanley, Acting Atty. General; and Melvin Purvis, head of the Chicago Bureau of Investigat.on in 1934. Purvis is reporting to his superiors on the slaying of John Dillinger. At far right, Thomas E. Dewey is sworn in as United States Attorney by Judge Frank Coleman.

a good one to the ambitious lawyer who recognized the political fact of life—that Schultz was connected with Tammany Hall boss James J. Hines.

Flashy and friendly, Davis defended Schultz against the federal government, but the bottom dropped out of his career when Schultz was murdered. Eventually, Davis testified against Hines, and was rewarded with only a one-year sentence to prison on a charge of conspiracy to operate the numbers racket. Upon his release, he wrote a series of articles about the birth of the syndicate, giving dates and figures and naming names: Lansky, Luciano, Lepke, and others. But no

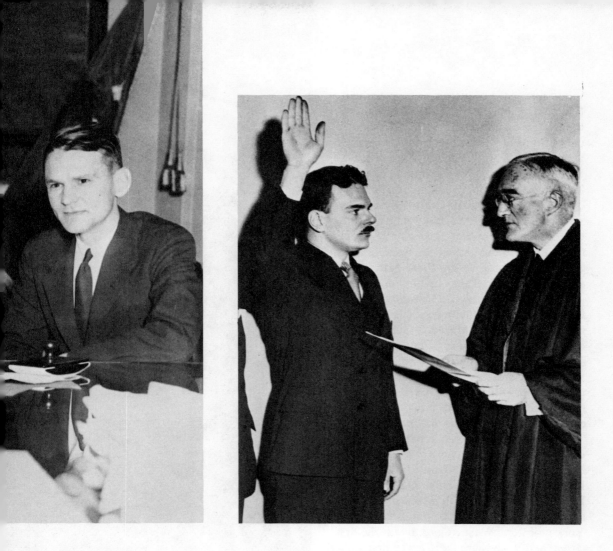

one was listening, and with his wife, former Follies showgirl Hope Dawn, he moved to California and was forgotten. On December 30, 1970, he died of a heart attack after holdup men robbed his home and threatened his wife and grandson. Dixie had never liked violence.

In essence, the National Crime Syndicate came about because intelligent men around the country wanted to hold on to what they had, and knew they could do so by cooperating with each other. It was the old Lansky-Torrio thesis: enough for all. Soon, however, came the "Big Heat," which forced a lot of gangsters to discover America where they realized for the first time the vast undeveloped potential remaining to be exploited.

Action breeds reaction, and political opportunity breeds politicians capable of taking advantage of that opportunity. In one sense the time was ripe for a crusader, and Thomas E. Dewey was eager to oblige. In another sense, Dewey, the ambitious politician, helped create the climate that demanded a crusader.

The banker, the baker, the candlestick maker were in disrepute following the crash in 1929. The many easy-money deals since made with gangsters had done little to restore public confidence. Under the smiling Roose-

velt, a new wave of idealism was generated.
It looked askance at the old order, at the
theory of a financial elite, at the idea that
the business of the country was business.
Some Republican critics, in fact, said the
whole New Deal was a communist plot,
but they were a minority. Roosevelt's attacks
on big-city bosses, while helping the crime
syndicate develop, did focus public opinion
on graft and corruption. Basically, however,
it was the very excesses of the twenties, so
gay and charming at the time, that in retro-
spect appeared so deserving of elimination.

J. Edgar Hoover, director of a reorganized
Federal Bureau of Investigation, read the
sentiments of the country and launched
attacks on the successors of Jesse James, the
independent free-booters who robbed banks
as much for kicks as for cash. While the FBI
chased John Dillinger and Alvin "Creepy"
Karpis, the real leaders of crime built a strong
empire with unlimited growth potential.

The pressure on the National Crime Syndicate, such as it was, came from Elmer Irey,
chief of the Intelligence Unit of the Bureau of
Internal Revenue, and Thomas E. Dewey.
Irey's men put Capone in prison in Chicago
and then opened a campaign against New
York mobsters. Waxey Gordon was the first
target, and it was here that Dewey first gained
public attention as the Assistant United States
Attorney who successfully prosecuted the tax
case against Waxey.

Dewey's godfather, so to speak, in his
professional career was George Z. Medalie,
the United States attorney who in March,
1931, persuaded the young lawyer to turn
to government service. Five months later
Dewey convicted Legs Diamond, the outlaw's
outlaw, but Legs was murdered while
appealing the sentence. On the other hand,
Dewey failed to convict Charles B. Mitchell,
former chairman of the National City Bank
and a prominent Republican. Was it a poor
case, or was the young lawyer looking ahead?
During the trial of Waxey Gordon in Novem-

At left, Al Capone with his
bodyguard Philip D'Andrea,
foreground. Capone usually traveled
around Chicago in a seven-ton
armored car. Above, Capone with
Jack "Legs" Diamond, one of New
York's busiest triggermen, during
the 1920s.

ber, 1933, Republican Medalie faced up to the realities of politics and resigned. Dewey got a conviction, and then resigned also. It seemed that his hopes of achieving political prestige through racket-busting were dead— at least until the Republicans regained power.

Not so. A state grand jury attempting to probe the numbers racket in New York City became annoyed at the lack of progress and demanded its own special prosecutor. Numbers was largely controlled by Dutch Schultz who had been well protected by Tammany Hall and Jimmy Hines. Presumably, suspecting the political angles, the regular district attorney wasn't eager to expose his party.

To assure an honest probe, Democratic Governor Herbert H. Lehman suggested four Republicans to conduct the grand jury investigation. Mysteriously, all declined, and by the process of elimination the job went to Dewey, the right man in the right place at the right time.

Dewey went after Hines, and convicted him. Schultz wasn't so easy. The "Feds" under Irey got him first, but one trial ended in a hung jury and the second in a verdict of acquittal. It was at this point that Murder, Inc. took over.

On October 23, 1935, Schultz was in the men's room at the Palace Chophouse in Newark, New Jersey. As he was washing his hands, his alleged assassin, Charles "The Bug" Workman, opened the door and fired one shot. Three of his aides were also gunned down. As Dutch lay dying, he remembered his mother and her high dreams. "Mother is the best bet and don't let Satan draw you too fast," he gasped.

Schultz was a man of quick and overpowering temper, as well as a mean and stingy nature, and there was little sorrow when he died. The big boys of the syndicate divided up his not inconsiderable empire. There was something for everyone; even the Cleveland Syndicate got a race track near Cincinnati— the one whose races Schultz had used to

"fix" the numbers racket payoff. The death of Dutch Schultz signaled the end of independent warfare and free-lance competition.

Cheated of Schultz, Dewey turned his guns on Lucky Luciano, generally considered to be the new capo of the "Italian Organization," as the Mafia was called in those days by those few with enough information to call it anything. Dewey acted in the knowledge that Mayor Fiorello La Guardia's first official act on taking office in 1934 was to order Luciano's arrest. He had no case, but the publicity stunt helped exaggerate Lucky's importance. Dewey was eager to play the same game, and between them they made Luciano into a monster instead of the business executive he considered himself to be. Dewey, however, intended to have a case when he made his arrest.

It took a year before Luciano was indicted as the vice boss of New York on ninety-one counts of extortion and compulsory prostitution. Lucky insisted he was framed, a sacrifice to Dewey's ambition, and his story has been confirmed in private by sources close to Dewey. In any case, the arrest helped Dewey win election in 1937 to the office of district attorney, giving him the title as well as the authority he had been exercising as special prosecutor. Had his ambitions stopped there it would have been a black day for the crime syndicate, but Dewey was aiming higher. He wanted to be President, and for that goal the office of governor of New York was a necessary preliminary.

If the conviction of Luciano opened the door for Dewey, it also gave Meyer Lansky an opportunity to bring the Mafia into closer cooperation with the National Crime Syndicate. Lansky, as Lucky's long-time friend and comrade, promised to get Luciano out of prison. Before departing to serve his sentence of thirty to fifty years, Lucky issued a final order to the Honored Society: "Cooperate with Meyer." Joe Adonis became the Mafia leader assigned to front for Lucky and

Dutch Schultz had three bodyguards —but they were not enough.

"Lucky" Luciano's luck ran out in 1936. He was convicted on so many counts that he was sentenced to 50 years. Above, Luciano, 2nd from right, is led from the court after sentencing. In 1946 he was paroled and deported to Italy, where he is shown at left. Several of his fellow gangsters gave him a farewell party aboard the ship, contemptuously ordering his guards to stand aside while baskets of food and wine were brought on board.

convey Lansky's orders, but the responsibility belonged to "the little guy," as Meyer was affectionately known. And "springing the boss" became the first item of business for the Mafia. It would take longer than was anticipated, thanks largely to unexpected developments like the Second World War, but eventually Lansky would keep his promise.

Dewey turned next to Lepke as the gangster whose conviction offered the greatest reward in terms of publicity and public service. As boss of the Syndicate's enforcement arm, he was an ideal target for ambitious politicians. The Federal Narcotics Bureau was after him as well, and even Hoover of the FBI issued a blast proclaiming Lepke "the most dangerous criminal in America." Hoover was no fool—he realized Dewey and Irey were hurting his image as the nation's number one crime-buster. Declaring that there could be no convictions if there were no witnesses, Lepke went into hiding and let the contract killers of Murder,

Inc., knock off those former friends he considered most dangerous. Something of a race developed to find Lepke before he eliminated all the witnesses. The hunt was literally world-wide, but during the months it lasted Lepke was still in New York.

This was the time of the "Big Heat," and it forced many gangsters to seek safety in remote parts of the country. Leaders, recognizing that gang-busting had become politically profitable in New York, began to look for new bases in the boondocks. Lansky began building an empire in Cuba. He had known the dictator, Fulgencio Batista, since Prohibition days and the two self-made men respected each other. Havana was something of a watering place for wealthy tourists and Lansky saw possibilities in gambling casinos as well as in the local race track. Lansky's partner, Bugsy Siegel, moved to Los Angeles to develop California and Nevada. Frank Costello, in partnership with Lansky and Kastel, made a deal with Huey Long and began big-scale gambling operations in New Orleans. Even the sands of Arizona were explored and preliminary investments made by a joint task force from New York and Cleveland.

That big cities were only a part of a big country, a small part, was something Lansky, Torrio, and a few others had known, but it came as a shock to many hoods who felt lost when they left the familiar haunts of New York, Boston, Philadelphia, Chicago, and Cleveland. Even so, many quickly adapted. They weren't ready for "the sands and lizards" of the Tucson area, as one hood described it, but they fell in love with the artificial glamour of Beverly Hills, and the Gold Coast of Florida. Hollywood, Florida, some twelve miles north of Miami Beach, became a favorite residential area, and many big-name gangsters bought or built homes there.

Capone had owned a home on Palm Island in Biscayne Bay, Miami Beach, for some years, and upon his release from prison he retired there. He died before realizing his

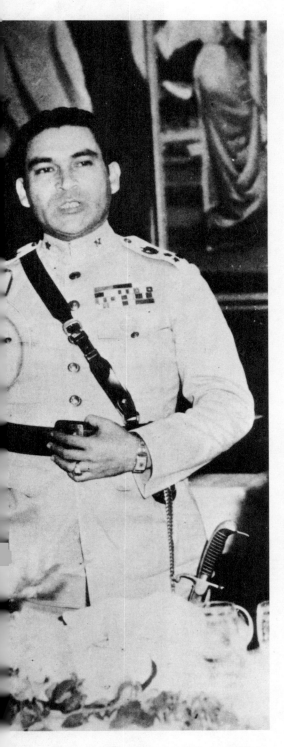

Dictator Fulgencio Batista of Cuba,
good friend of Meyer Lansky.
Seated, Federico Laredo Bru,
vice-president.

plan to buy acceptance in the area as a philanthropist, but others in years to come were to be more successful with the ploy. The gangsters who were first of all good businessmen soon recognized the potential for development in resort areas and began investing their surplus cash in land, hotels, and nightclubs. Local business executives, still hurting for money, welcomed the investments as a mark of confidence in the future of the community. No one felt inclined to look deeply into the source of an investor's wealth. Money bought instant respectability.

Bootleg cash, made in the big cities, was scattered about the country as seed money. In time this would produce not only immense profits but an accompanying quota of corruption that, in turn, would bring more crime. The pincers might be closing around Lepke, but crime was taking root and the fate of one individual was not important.

So it was that when the hunt for Lepke became too intense, when it began to interfere too much with normal operations and projected expansion, the Syndicate's board of directors took action. Reluctantly, perhaps, but without serious disagreement except from Anastasia, board members voted to sacrifice their old comrade to the common good.

Lepke was given a simple choice—surrender and make the best deal you can, or be rubbed out.

Lansky convinced Lepke that he could get off easiest by giving himself up to the Feds. The man who argued the hardest against this was the holdout on the board, Albert Anastasia. Lepke was Big Albert's hero. Anastasia had entered the United States illegally in 1917 and developed his muscle on the Brooklyn docks. He became the leader of a Brooklyn gang of thugs who sold their service of violence to anyone who could pay. Joe Adonis made much use of Anastasia and gave him a boost up the syndicate ladder. But Anastasia's loyalties were with Lepke.

During the Big Heat, he made himself personally responsible for Lepke's comfort and safety. He blamed Lansky for Lepke's decision to surrender and this created a vendetta that ultimately caused a major crisis in Syndicate-Mafia relations and abruptly ended Anastasia's career. With help from newspaper columnist Walter Winchell, Lepke surrendered to J. Edgar Hoover on the night of August 24, 1939, and the Big Heat was over. Hoover had no use for Lepke—a warrant charging him with interstate flight to avoid prosecution was worthless since Lepke had not left town. The prisoner was turned over to the Federal Narcotics Bureau, however, and that agency convicted him. But it was Burton Turkus, the assistant district attorney of Brooklyn, who broke Murder, Inc., wide open and sent Lepke to the electric chair for murder.

Lepke remains the only major gang leader to be officially executed by any state in a half-century of syndicate activity. In contrast, Lansky thought he was unlucky when forced to spend three months in a New York prison in 1953. Again the lesson here is the inevitability of change and the necessity of adapting to new conditions. Lepke, a smart man in the twenties, relied too long on terror. Lansky, an even smarter man, stayed in the shadows, anticipating events and occasionally helping them happen. He did not grieve long for Lepke, a friend since early manhood, for Lepke had only himself to blame for his troubles. A man of self-discipline and limited appetites, Lansky profited by the weaknesses he found in others and in society. A man could turn any situation to his advantage if he was smart enough, Lansky believed, and the Big Heat was no exception.

Nor was the probe of Murder, Inc., although to many hoods it seemed the end of the world. It all started early in 1940 when Harry Rudolph, a minor and somewhat unstable hood who had been brooding about the "execution" of one of his friends in a

The end of the road for Lepke, shown here arriving from New York City Federal House of Detention at the Court of Appeals in Albany in 1943. The detective is taking no chances. Lepke was accused of being responsible for more than 20 murders. He was 43 years old when executed.

144

gang war years before, finally found someone to listen to him. Assistant District
Attorney Burton Turkus didn't take the tale
too seriously, but it gave him a chance to
pick up three hoods and get them off the
streets. One of the three was Abe "Kid Twist"
Reles, an old member of the Bugs and Meyer
Mob who had graduated to high rank in the
new enforcement organization.

For years gangsters had been squealing
to Dewey's office in return for immunity, and
Reles—once he was bluffed into believing he
might be in serious trouble—decided to try
the same gambit with Turkus. It worked, and
Reles began to sing. Once he had violated the
underworld code, his only safety lay in
putting the finger on everyone, so his song
went on and on and on—for twelve days. He
gave full details of eighty-five murders and
information about a thousand others.

At least three high-ranking members of the
syndicate were implicated directly by Reles:
Lepke, Bugsy Siegel, and Albert Anastasia.
Lepke, as noted, went to the chair. Siegel
was arrested but beat the rap when the
principal witness, Reles, died suddenly. And
despite a boast that a "perfect murder case"
existed against Anastasia, he was never
indicted. Turkus did his best, but his boss,
District Attorney William O'Dwyer, was
ambitious and the Italian vote had become
important in New York elections. (That, at
least, is the kinder theory.)

Details of Murder, Inc., caused a sensation
when made public, but as usual, the full
implications were not easily understood. The
public, getting its information from the press
which, in turn, depended on public officials,
confused the enforcement arm of the Syndicate with the Syndicate itself, and Murder,
Inc., came to mean the entire apparatus. In
the same way, twenty years later the Mafia
became in the minds of many synonymous
with organized crime. Thus it was assumed
that with the cracking of the murder gang,
the entire Syndicate had been broken and

Canary Abe "Kid Twist" Reles, who
began his criminal career at 13,
above left, with Irving Goldstein.
Reles was Bugsy Siegel's bodyguard
at one time. When he decided to
sing, he filled 25 stenographer's
notebooks and either solved
outright or gave clues to 1,000
murders. Above far right is the Half
Moon Hotel in Coney Island, where
Reles fell to his death while
guarded by five policemen. Out the
window with him went Assistant
District Attorney Burton Turkus'
case against Albert Anastasia.
Turkus, left and a colleague,
Solomon Klien, are shown in picture
at right.

could be forgotten. What's more, since Dewey had become identified with gang-busting in New York, it was assumed by most of the country that he was responsible for the successful probe. Many years later when Dewey died, several major newspapers such as the Miami *Herald* listed among his accomplishments the destruction of Murder, Inc.

In reality, the loss of its enforcement arm helped the Syndicate more than it harmed it. The kill-on-contract boys had been necessary in the early days of the Syndicate, when there were still independents such as Schultz, and room for disagreement over territorial alignments. The elimination of strong personalities like Luciano and Lepke made it easier to control the rest without the threat of violence. Lansky's power was growing all the while not because of the troops he could command but because he was showing other gang leaders how to get rich, and permitting them to share the wealth. The bribe had long

before replaced the bullet where politicians and police officers were concerned; it was now to become the chief instrument of internal discipline as well.

As far as the syndicate was concerned, the Murder, Inc., investigation was a good show for the squares in that it satisfied their capacity for moral indignation and reassured them that in the long run crime didn't pay. They could go back to sleep for another decade or so.

Abe Reles, the canary who could sing but couldn't fly, was tossed out the window of the Half Moon Hotel, where he had been guarded by picked men and steel doors, on November 12, 1941. Less than a month later, the Japanese bombed Pearl Harbor and the attention of the nation turned from the enemy within to the enemy without.

The war, among other things, would enable Lansky to keep his promise to "spring" Luciano.

5 THE CASINO ERA

Even prior to Pearl Harbor tourism had taken a dive and Meyer Lansky closed his casino at the Hotel Nacional in Havana. You can't live off the Cuban people, he explained.

That was to be the problem in the United States after Pearl Harbor. You couldn't live, at least in suitable Syndicate style, off the local yokels. A few "rug joints," catering to the very rich, continued to operate, and cheap bust-out joints such as those in Phenix City Alabama, stayed open to help service men spend their money. Essentially, however, the big plans made by Lansky and his friends had to be postponed until after the war. Meanwhile, there was the black market to think about. Plenty of money to be made there. And, with war's end, would come perhaps the same sort of reaction that followed the First World War as a lot of people tried to make up for lost opportunities. Then would be the time for casinos.

Among those planning for that happy day were Lansky's old allies in the Cleveland Syndicate. Moe Dalitz and company had been operating casinos in and around Cleveland for several years, the most lavish being

the Mounds Club. Following Dutch Schultz's murder in 1935 they took over the Coney Island Race Track on the north side of the Ohio River outside Cincinnati and renamed it River Downs. They also invested in several small casinos in the area, such as the Arrowhead Club which Sam "Gameboy" Miller, the group's efficient troubleshooter, soon had operating. But the view across the muddy Ohio was fascinating. Newport and Covington were two small cities cut off from the rest of Kentucky by a range of hills as well as less tangible but just as real ethnic and cultural factors. The area had been known as "Little Mexico" back in Prohibition days, a place where the only law was a man's shooting iron, and it was still as corrupt as George Remus, king of the bootleggers, had left it. In fact, some of Remus's former lieutenants including Peter Schmidt and Buck Brady had become important figures in Newport gambling. Schmidt had the most ambitious place, the Beverly Hills Club east of town on the road to Frankfort. It was huge and plush, and was beginning to draw business from Cincinnati and other Ohio

149

towns. Brady's place, the Primrose Club in Wilder, a suburb even tougher than Newport proper, was just a glorified bust-out joint. It could wait. The key to Kentucky was obviously Schmidt, for the stubborn old Dutchman didn't want to sell.

Using local talent, the Syndicate arranged to burn down the Beverly Hills Club. A young girl, daughter of the caretaker who lived on the premises in the off season, was killed. Still Schmidt resisted. He rebuilt the club on an even more lavish scale, and his reopening was attended by the governors of three states. But the Syndicate had the cash, and the "ding-donging," as local gangsters called it, continued. Eventually, Schmidt had trouble hiring reliable "muscle" to guard his bankroll and protect his customers. He was reduced to hiring Negroes. In the eyes of many first-generation Americans, who needed someone lower on the pecking order to despise, equipping Negroes with submachine guns was not only dangerous but an insult as well.

By 1940, Schmidt had been convinced. The Syndicate moved in, remodeled the Beverly Hills Club, and began bringing in top stars from Hollywood and Broadway. It became "the Showplace of the Nation," and most citizens of the area were quite proud of it.

The conquest of the Beverly was but the opening wedge. Sam Tucker was appointed branch manager for the Syndicate, and under his direction the Lookout House in nearby Covington was acquired. Jimmy Brink, the owner, did not resist and was left with a small piece of the action. He had pretensions to being a Kentucky gentleman and horse-breeder, and he named Tucker as "the gentleman of the boys" from Cleveland. Smaller casinos in downtown Covington and Newport were also easily acquired. Only Brady put up a fight before surrendering the Primrose. After a shootout on the street that left two wrecked cars and the wounded body of a Syndicate enforcer, Brady was found

Top, A. B. "Happy" Chandler at his inauguration as governor of Kentucky. Above, Sam Tucker, charter member of the Cleveland Syndicate. Right, James Brink with his Derby entry, Red Devil.

150

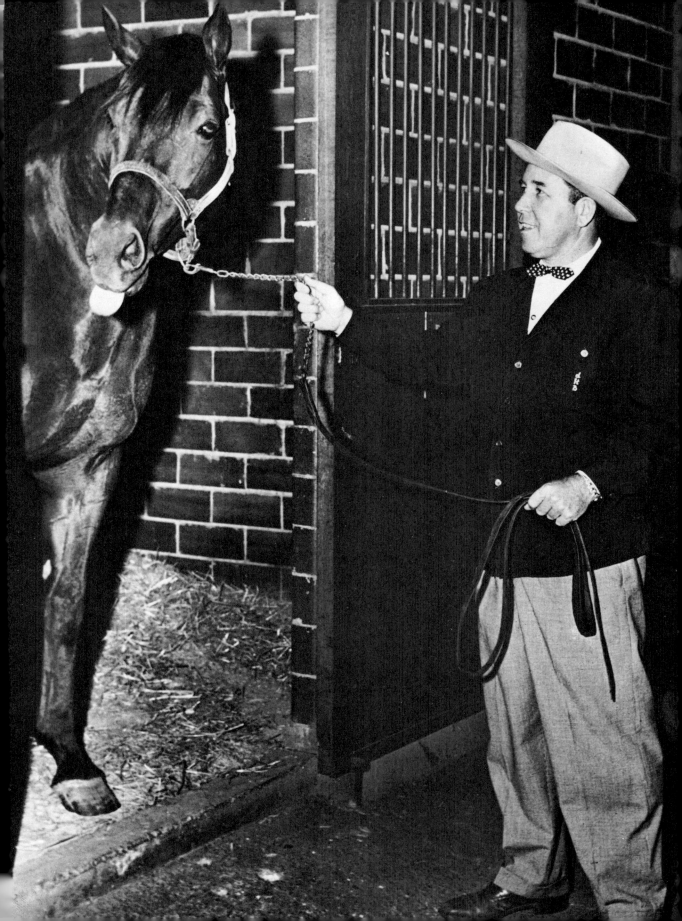

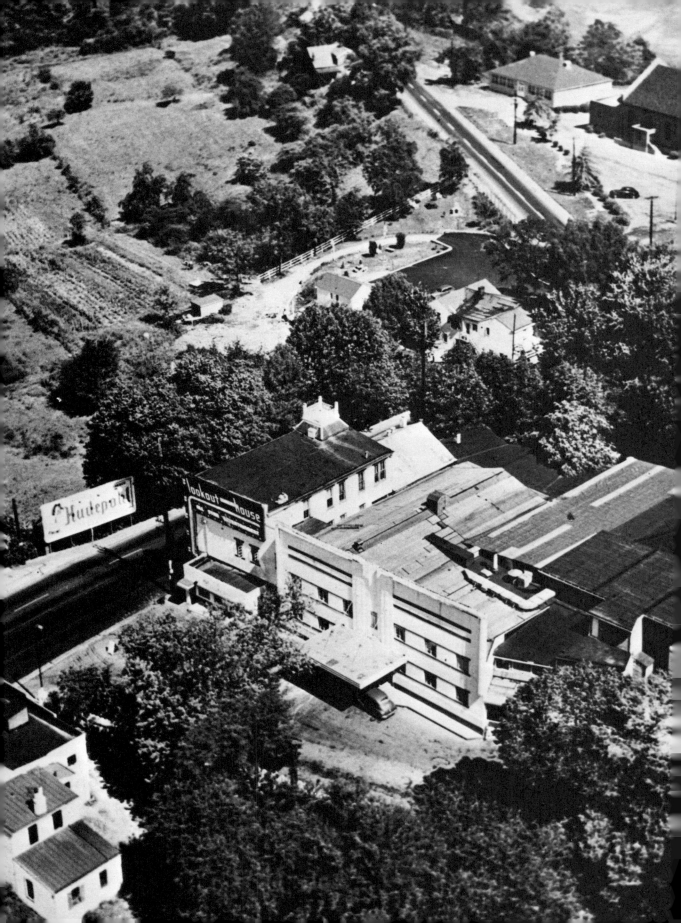

"Brink's Bungalow,"
home of Jimmy Brink.
After his death in
1952, it became a
guest house for
visiting gamblers.
"Gil the Brain"
Beckley often stayed here.

On opposite page is
Lookout House in
Covington, Ky., a
favorite nightspot for
Cincinnati
businessmen looking
for action. At left, an
interior shot after a
state police raid.

Hidey-hole at the Hi-De-Ho Club. In a 1951 state police raid of the establishment near Wilder, Ky., outside Newport, Ky., the girls were discovered hiding in a secret room.

with a small arsenal hiding in a nearby privy. He had been out hunting, he explained. Impressed, the Syndicate paid him well to retire to Florida.

Casino gambling was strictly illegal in Kentucky, but the Syndicate joints operated as openly as grocery stores or cafés. Soon after taking over the Beverly, the mob installed a group of county officials in Newport who served for twenty years or more without a serious problem. On the state level, political contributions bought local autonomy. Governor A. B. "Happy" Chandler was not speaking for himself alone when he proclaimed "the right of the people of Newport to have it dirty" if they desired.

At intervals the Syndicate tried to curtail prostitution and bust-out gambling, knowing

full well that if a rebellion began it would be due to local indignation over immoral conditions. But here, for once, the big boys were largely helpless. The area had too many people for tight control, and cops accustomed to taking bribes for casino gambling saw no reason why they shouldn't also take from madams and bust-out operators. Prostitution, however, did become rather tightly organized into day and night houses. The day houses were largely for the benefit of area business-men who wanted a "quickie" on their lunch hour, or before going home to the wife after work. The night houses opened about dark and catered to convention visitors to Cincin-nati and young sports from Louisville and Indianapolis. Tradition had it that no virgin could be offered to the trade until the New-

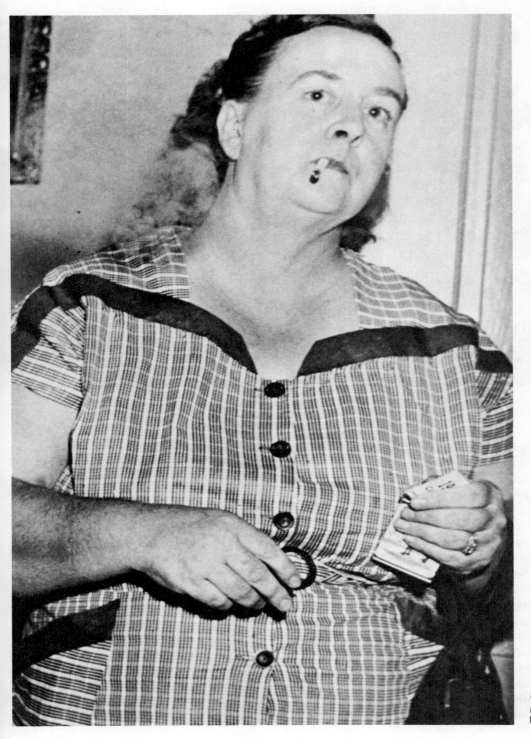

"Big Ruth" Jarvis,
madam at the
Hi-De-Ho Club.

port police chief had a chance to "inspect" her. Since most of the brothels were located within a three-block radius of the police station, he didn't have far to go. Whenever a civic group would complain about conditions they were reminded of the Beverly Hills Club, the big-name entertainment it offered, and the money it brought in. The fleas came with the dog, the people agreed.

So the Cleveland Syndicate expanded at a time when prices were low and public attention diverted, building for the postwar period when, it was hoped, history would repeat itself. Others were building too. Bugsy Siegel, who had gone to Los Angeles during the Big Heat, had his eyes on Las Vegas. Legal gambling was not necessarily more profitable or safer than the illegal kind (one

still had to make sure the political situation remained favorable) but it did offer one unique advantage—a chance to become respectable. The boys who began as bootleggers were approaching middle age, and respectability now appealed. Moreover, operating from a legal base it might be possible to conceal all kinds of illegal activity. So, in consultation with Lansky, Bugsy was exploring the grubby town in southern Nevada. Unlike Reno to the north, it was within easy driving distance of metropolitan Los Angeles.

Owney Madden had already achieved respectability. He had killed to many men for the new order of things in New York. The Syndicate permitted him to go into exile in Hot Springs, Arkansas, an isolated but popular resort and hideout. Luciano was

State police give the heave-ho to the slot machines at the Hi-De-Ho Club. At left, a Newport, Ky., family-style tavern of the 1940s.

there, for instance, when Dewey secured his indictment, and it took a detachment of Arkansas Rangers to extract him from the protective clutches of Hot Springs cops. Madden had married the daughter of a local politician and settled down to provide entertainment facilities for visiting hoods as well as the gouty rich who came there to bathe in the healing waters. Handbooks, where bets on horse races and other sports events were taken, and small casinos were the principal sources of entertainment, but Madden believed the place had greater possibilities and was waiting for the war to end to begin a development program. Lansky was willing to provide additional funds as needed.

Other opportunities existed in New Orleans, Saratoga Springs, and of course on the Gold Coast of Florida, but Lansky was soon involved in one of the most bizarre episodes in the history of the Second World War. "Operation Underworld," it was called, and it was to provide him with the excuse he needed to spring Luciano from prison.

The ambitious Dewey took time out from his pursuit of Lepke to run for governor of New York on the Republican ticket in 1938. He won the nomination but lost the election. Lansky was disappointed; it was vital to his plans for Lucky that Dewey become the state's chief executive. He had a bad scare in 1940 when Dewey struck boldly at his real objective—the Presidency. But Wendell Willkie, a very dark horse, ran off with the prize at the Republican national convention. Two years later, Dewey ran successfully for governor after promising not to seek the Presidency in 1944. Frank Hogan took over as district attorney and made it into a lifetime job.

Operation Underworld began in 1942, before Dewey's election but after it was apparent he would win in a walk. Allegedly, Naval Intelligence needed Luciano's aid in protecting the docks of New York and New

Moses Polakoff, attorney for Lucky Luciano.

Jersey from agents of Germany and Italy. Only Lucky had sufficient prestige to command the Mafia, which virtually ruled the docks, to cooperate. Naturally, in such an emergency, the Navy turned to Dewey's office. Moses Polakoff, who had served both Luciano and Lansky as an attorney and was a personal friend of Lansky as well, was consulted. He insisted that Lansky was the only man who could persuade Luciano to cooperate. Lansky was allowed to see Lucky who, of course, was cooperative—when he understood what was happening. Orders went out to the Mafia to cooperate with Lansky who was cooperating with the Navy in order to spring the boss.

What this achieved is uncertain. There was no episode of sabotage on the docks reported, but whether the Mafia or the FBI was responsible is a matter of some dispute. Both, in fact, took the credit.

Luciano was also credited by some with making possible the Allied invasion of Sicily, although, again, he had rivals. Nicola Gentile, that exiled Mafia troubleshooter, thought he did more than anyone else to arrange a soft landing.

In 1971, Lansky was in Israel trying hard to persuade officials that he should be allowed to live there. As part of his campaign he gave an interview which was printed in an Israeli paper. An English version was sent to the United States, but unhappily the story suffered somewhat in translation. Here is Lansky's recollection of "Operation Under-world" as he looked back from Tel Aviv:

"When Italy entered the Second World War there was a feeling that some Italians are not patriotic enough. The Intelligence Branch of the American Navy was afraid that those Italians working on the docks, or Italian fishermen using their boats, might collaborate with the enemy . . . Mr. Hogan was then district attorney in Manhattan. He called the lawyer of Charlie 'Lucky' Luciano —Mr. Moe Polakoff. Said Hogan: 'You are

Journal NEW YORK **American**

AN AMERICAN PAPER FOR THE AMERICAN PEOPLE

No. 20,278—DAILY   MONDAY, JULY 12, 1943

7TH SPORTS RACING

O SICILY TOWNS FALL TO ALLIES

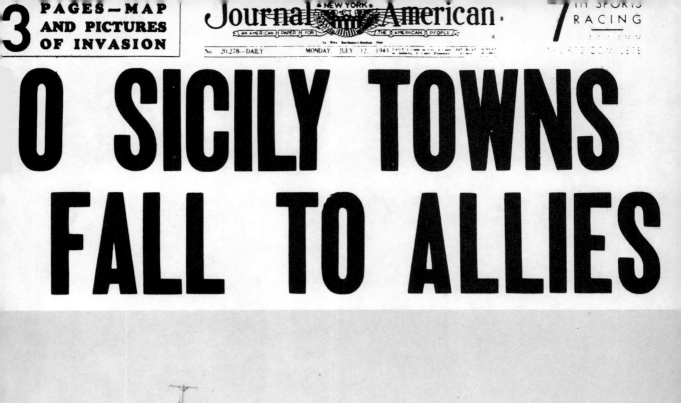

ALLIES SEIZE 100-MI. SICILY AREA, SMASH INLAND IN FIERCE BATTLE; LANDINGS SUCCEED—EISENHOWER

KS MOVING

By Richard Tregaskis, International News Service Staff Correspondent

NORTH AFRICA, Allied Headquarters, July 10.—A swelling tide

In 1947 Lucky Luciano. violating
his parole, went to Cuba. Meyer
Lansky saw him there. When the
Kefauver Committee asked what
they talked about, he said, "Purely
social. What else could I talk to him
about?" Frank Costello also met
Luciano in Havana; they talked
about "his health and what not."
Here Lucky is shown leaving Cuba.

the lawyer of Charles Lucky, so go to him and see if he might be helpful.' Lucky was then in prison. Polakoff answered that he wants to go there with me and with Frank Costello. The next morning Polakoff took me to the D.A. who explained the situation to me. I went immediately to see Frank Costello, telling him the story and asking him what does he feel about it. Frank was patriotic and felt that help should be given. So we made a white lie and we decided that we will tell Charlie Lucky that if he will be helpful in this case it might help him to get him out of prison . . . Charlie Lucky was corporative [sic] and he sent some words immediately to his men, telling him that he will appreciate it if they will follow his directions because it might help him a lot. Charlie Lucky was much respected in the labor unions and they respected his words. . ."

As to the invasion of Sicily, Lansky told his interviewer:

"The Navy asked me to collect as many pictures and postcards of Sicily, in order to study its topography, from the private albums of Italian immigrants. I volunteered to do it and I remember how many Italians we gathered in the Navy Office in Church Street in New York. The office was stuffed with Sicilians. I also operated upon official request in organizing informers in certain areas in New York for reporting against espionage activities in the German-immigrant neighborhoods. After the war the authorities forgot these activities of mine and others."

Lansky was perhaps being unfair in 1971. The suspicion existed for many years that in return for his services he had been promised immunity from federal prosecution just as Luciano was promised parole. If so, it would seem that his collection of Sicilian postcards paid off rather handsomely. It should be noted, however, that his statement involves Costello in Operation Underworld for the first time. Even the accounts given the Kefauver Committee in 1951 made no mention of

Costello. Not for nothing was Frank known as "the Politician."

In any event, Luciano was rewarded for his alleged war services. Early in 1946, he was paroled from prison and deported to Italy. Lansky, Costello, and a gaggle of politicians saw him off at the docks where longshoremen kept newspapermen at bay by force. Shortly thereafter, Luciano slipped into Cuba and tried to operate as capo di capi re from that vantage point. The United States government put on pressure—something it was reluctant to do two decades later when Lansky went to Israel—and Luciano was forced to return to Italy. Before departing, he ordered the Mafia to obey Lansky who, in effect, became acting boss of the Honored Society. Patriotism had paid off for Lansky as well.

During this period, other members of the Mafia were having their problems as well. On March 18, 1943, a federal grand jury indicted leading members of the Chicago Syndicate: Frank Nitti, Phil D'Andrea, Paul Ricca, John Rosselli, and several others. They were charged with conspiracy to obtain money by extortion from persons engaged in interstate commerce. The persons so engaged were in the movie-making, and showing, business.

Back in 1935, the Syndicate, spearheaded by the Chicago boys who gained control of a key union, moved in on Hollywood. They shook down the big producers for hundreds of thousands of dollars, and took more thousands from distributors across the country. Perhaps a contributing factor in the shakedown was the movie-makers' experience with gangster films, an important staple since the success of *Scarface* and *Little Caesar*. They believed their own stories. When Bugsy Siegel appeared as the Syndicate's western representative, he was made into a celebrity by the scared fat cats of Hollywood. Another associate of Lansky, Longie Zwillman, invested a lot of money in such pictures as *Guest Wife*. Professing to be deeply in love with Jean Harlow, he tried to buy pubic hair allegedly cut off when she had an emergency appendectomy.

But the 1943 indictment was too realistic a slice of life for Frank "the Enforcer" Nitti. He had served one term for tax evasion and didn't like it. So he killed himself. The others went to prison and were paroled for good behavior after serving one-third of their ten year sentences. That created another scandal, but the boys still went free.

During the war, the big dough was to be made in war contracts and in supplying the home front with black-market items. The experience of Prohibition proved most useful, and once again liquor was smuggled into the country on a big scale. "Warehouse receipts," the wartime equivalent of "permits for withdrawal," became exceedingly valuable. History more or less repeated itself. Liquor was in short supply and many of those holding it demanded prices far in excess of the legal limits set by the Office of Price Administration.

One episode involved Batista, dictator of Cuba and friend of Lansky. The plan was to take a small amount of good bourbon and blend it with a lot of cheap Cuban rum to produce a bastard drink to be sold as "blended" whiskey. A supply of whiskey barrels in which bourbon had been aged was shipped to Havana. It was discovered that if the rum was put in the barrels and left for a few days in hot sunlight before being rolled downhill to the dock, it took on some of the characteristics of bourbon. Nothing need be added.

Batista, who owned the rum, offered to transport the sun-blended whiskey-rum to Florida, and made available his yacht, an old American gunboat. Then, after getting it on board, he demanded $10,000 more for the rum.

Eventually the stuff reached the Cedar Valley Distillery at Wooster, Ohio, where it

Frank Nitti, Capone associate, who handled most of the protection money, is seen above in 1930. At right, Nitti's body in 1943. The same day a federal indictment was returned charging Nitti and others with violation of the Federal Anti-Racketeering Act, he took his own life near his home in Riverside, Ill.

Inn, the Club Greenacres, the Club Boheme to the north around Gulfstream Park in Broward County. Fancy casinos blossomed along the Mississippi Gulf Coast at Biloxi, and the Beverly Club outside New Orleans was the flagship of a Jefferson Parish gambling empire. In New Jersey near the bridge to New York City, a huge casino operated unmolested, and to the north at Sarotaga Springs, the racing crowd was given indoor action at several famous spots.

In Las Vegas, Bugsy Siegel had not waited a moment longer than necessary. At a time when veterans couldn't get material for housing, Bugsy called upon the black market resources of the Syndicate to begin construction of the Flamingo on the road to Los Angeles. The area would soon be known as "the Strip" after Siegel's dream proved practical. Encouraging him was his girl friend, Virginia Hill, who may have considered herself "the world's best lay," but who never so boasted, contrary to enduring legend. The Cleveland Syndicate called off plans to build a huge casino-hotel at White Sulphur Springs, Virginia, and instead took over the Desert Inn. Dandy Phil Kastel left New Orleans to the care of Carlos Marcello and Seymour Weiss, and built the Tropicana as a monument for his love, a girl he had found in the French Quarter.

Other gangsters joined the gold rush to the land of legal gambling, but ironically, Siegel didn't live to enjoy his triumph. On the night of June 20, 1947, he was blasted by a Syndicate gunman as he sat in the living room of Virginia's borrowed Beverly Hills home. The high-powered bullets knocked out his right eye.

Investigators at first toyed with the idea that Siegel was executed because he was on the wrong side of the so-called "Wire-Service

Benjamin "Bugsy" Siegel got his nickname because he was hotheaded, but few dared call him that to his face. Above, his Las Vegas nightclub.

10 CENTS

Journal American

AN AMERICAN FOR THE AMERICAN PEOPLE

This Paper in Two Sections - Also Colored Comic and Magazine

No. 21,691—DAILY   SATURDAY, JUNE 21, 1947

7TH SPOR
RACIN
★★★★★
SPORTS COMPLE

'BUGSIE' SIEGEL KILLED BY GANG

ees New U.S.
Gasoline, Oil
xport Curbs

y RAYMOND WILCOVE
National News Service Sta

N. Y. Mobster Mowed Down On Coast

(Fu   Photos Other

Filibuster Stalls Vote On Veto

Siegel tried to buy class at every opportunity. In California, he picked "nice classy neighbors" like Anita Louise and Sonja Henie before he built his $150,000 house. Terribly vain, his clothes were monogrammed down to his silk shorts. He wore an elastic chin strap to bed to keep his profile from sagging. He once told a fearful acquaintance, "There's no chance you'll get killed. We only kill each other."

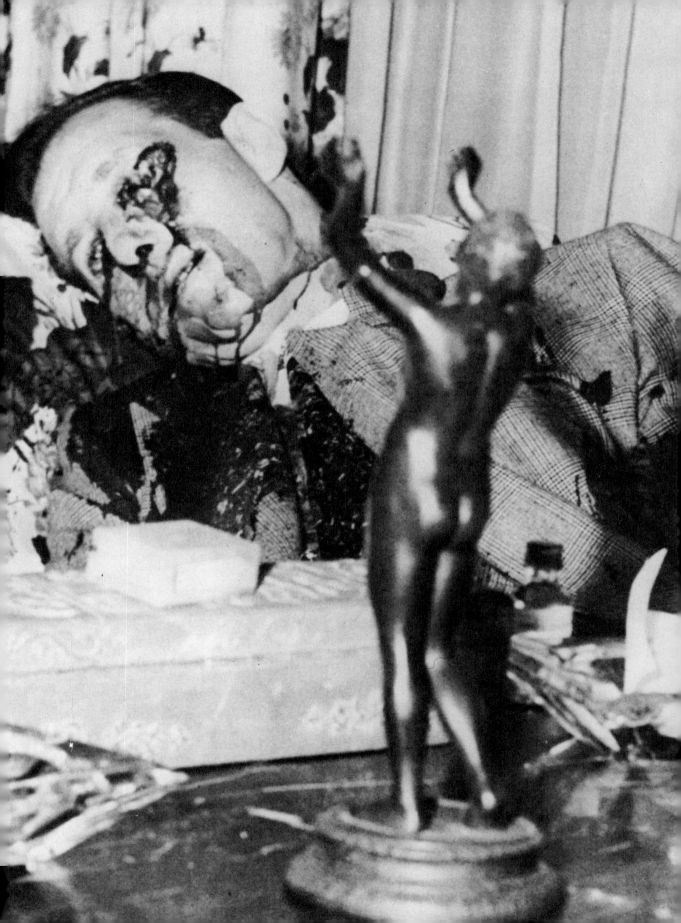

Appearing before the Kefauver Committee, Frank Costello was carefully and conservatively dressed. The only flamboyant touch was a white handkerchief in his breast pocket embroidered with his name in large red script. When asked why he had become an American citizen, he said, "Because I love this country."

War," a battle for control of Nationwide News Service that supplied illegal handbooks around the country with essential racing data on odds and winners. But that whole affair was peanuts compared to the potential take from the Flamingo. Siegel was killed, it was later discovered, because he was planning to cheat his colleagues in the syndicate who had put up much of the money for the expensive resort casino.

It was the first time that a member of the board of directors was ordered killed, but it was not the last. The syndicate took charge of the Flamingo, and in 1971 Lansky was among several men indicted for conspiring to skim $36 million of untaxed casino profits from it. Truly, Siegel had created a horn of plenty on the sands of Nevada.

Action, reaction. By 1950, the stink of corruption was beginning to drown out the sweet smell of success. Republicans, bitterly disappointed when Harry S. Truman upset Dewey in 1948, were probing for issues even as the Democrats had done in the 1920s. The Truman scandals were neither as far-reaching nor as vast as the Harding scandals —can a deep-freeze compare to Teapot Dome?—but they helped set the new mood of the country. And in 1950 came Senator Estes Kefauver, a young man from Tennessee, who somehow persuaded his colleagues that a sweeping probe of organized crime in interstate commerce was needed. Kefauver had some experience with crime and corruption; to win office he had defeated the "Boss Crump" machine in his home state. He assembled a group of dedicated young men, inspiring them with the knowledge that circumstances had provided a good opportunity to make an important contribution. Most Senate investigations simply harrow ground already plowed; Kefauver's team determined to break new ground. Such men as Joseph L. Nellis, who headed up the probe of the Cleveland Syndicate, produced an amazing amount of new

information in a very short time.

The hearings became a television sensation—so much so that some of the gangsters who "starred" in the show must have had mixed emotions. Men like Lansky and Costello had invested heavily in the new industry. Consolidated Television was only one such investment. Often, however, the gangsters put their personal welfare ahead of their investments and refused to talk unless television cameras were turned off.

Committee investigators followed the trail back to Prohibition and exposed the strange alliance of crime, politics, and big business that had evolved since Black Tuesday, 1929. In city after city, the working relationships were disclosed. The existence of the Mafia— not as a huge, controlling organization, but as a "cement" holding together scattered interests—was confirmed. "Operation Underworld" was brought out, at least partially, into the sunlight, and the Newport-Covington area's connections with syndicated crime were revealed. From Las Vegas, where Siegel's murder was studied, to Miami Beach, where the probe centered on the Chicago Syndicate's attempt to muscle in on a local outfit known as the S and G Syndicate, the sordid story unfolded. But was anyone listening?

The public followed the drama much as they followed soap-opera serials. Somehow, it all seemed too unreal to a generation brainwashed into believing that the FBI had eliminated gangsters and that politicians who said the right things about Flag and Mother-hood could do no real wrong. Across the country a number of citizens' crime commissions were set up and a few newspapers gave reporters the title of "crime editor," but the interest faded as quickly as it had developed.

Senator Joseph McCarthy, gathering strength if not solid data since 1948, gradually took the headlines away from Kefauver, and much of America breathed a

Joe Adonis upon his release from Prison in 1953.

DEALER MUST HIT SOFT 17

sigh of relief. Somehow it *felt* more patriotic to be up in arms against Red traitors than to be fighting to expose fellow Americans who, after all, had just been a little too free with their enterprise. In the uproar over McCarthyism, the findings of the Kefauver Committee were largely forgotten.

Yet there were some tangible achievements. Frank Costello became useless to the Syndicate as a result of the publicity picturing him as the "Prime Minister of the Underworld." Lansky was forced to shutter his illegal casinos along the Gold Coast of Florida. And Joe Adonis's background finally caught up with him. For years he had deluded investigators into believing he had been born in the United States whereas actually, he came to New York from Italy at the age of seven. In 1956, facing a perjury rap and realizing that the truth of his birthplace was at last known, he accepted deportation to Italy.

Although action went on in Newport, Hot Springs, Gretna (New Orleans), Youngstown, Cicero, Biloxi, Beaumont, etc., and Las Vegas continued its fantastic growth, the loss of Florida was a serious blow. A regional gambling center was needed for the area. Lansky, looking ahead, could see that open, illegal, casino gambling within the states was too risky, too subject to an attack of virtue by citizens or politicians. Eventually, perhaps, there could be new islands of legality created, but until then it would be best to go elsewhere. The automobile had given the gangsters of Prohibition great mobility, permitting interstate operations. Now the plane, which already had brought thousands of suckers to Las Vegas, could take the same squares to other exotic places. Cuba was convenient, familiar, and cooperative. But, for security, it needed stability. Batista had been forced to permit free elections in 1944 and had been defeated. He had retired to Florida, but was eager to return to power. Lansky decided to back him. In short order, less than a year after Kefauver's committee disbanded, Batista was again dictator of Cuba, and Lansky began building a new and greater gambling empire.

Nevada gaming agents and employees of the Silver Slipper Casino, one of the oldest clubs on the Las Vegas Strip, are shown closing down a crap table following a raid. State gaming authorities halted gambling at the club because of alleged cheating with crooked dice.

NEW YORK
Journal American
FR — AN AMERICAN PAPER FOR THE AMERICAN PEOPLE

No. 25.402—DAILY   FRIDAY, OCTOBER 25, 1957   10 Cents

7TH SPORTS RACING
Bid and Asked
SPORTS COMPLETE

MURDER INC. GANG CHIEF SLAIN IN BARBER'S CHAIR

Report Ike May Attend Europe Talk

WASHINGTON, Oct. 25 (AP).—A possible Allied summit conference which could take President Eisenhower to Europe in the next few months was reported to have been discussed during the Eisenhower-Macmillan talks ending today. The idea arose, it was reported, as...

MOVE CLOCKS BACK SUNDAY

Don't forget that Sunday at 2 a.m. you set the clock back an hour, if you want to be in step with also tomorrow as Daylight Saving Time comes to an...

New York and the northeastern section of the U.S. as well as a few other areas are last to go back to standard time, other sections having reverted Oct. 20.

Remember you move the clock BACK an hour to 1 a.m. Sunday.

Rocket Up 4,000 Mi., U.S. Claims

WASHINGTON, Oct. 25 (AP)—Air Force officers who conducted "Project Far Side" expressed belief today that one of the rockets... a balloon...

2 Kill Anastasia In 7th Ave. Hotel

Life Story on Page 13

By ARTHUR McCLURE

Albert Anastasia, Lord High Executioner of Brooklyn's infamous Murder, Inc., was shot to death in gangland style today as he was getting a haircut in the barbershop of the Park Sheraton.

Two masked gunmen... 7th ave. and 55th... ber's...

Havana became the Las Vegas of the Caribbean. The Syndicate poured millions into new skyscraper hotel casinos that changed the skyline, and the city boomed with every racket known to man. As usual, Lansky allowed others to share the wealth while retaining control, thanks to his personal friendship with the dictator. As usual, some members of the Mafia weren't satisfied and wanted more. Albert Anastasia, for one. Rebuffed, he provoked a crisis in the syndicate by challenging Lansky's power. Marshaling his forces around the country, Lansky easily defeated Anastasia's efforts, and when Albert persisted and called a meeting of other dissatisfied Mafia members, he ordered his execution. Anastasia was murdered on October 25, 1957, in the barber shop of the same hotel where twenty-nine years earlier Arnold "the Brain" Rothstein had been hit. Reporters who made much of

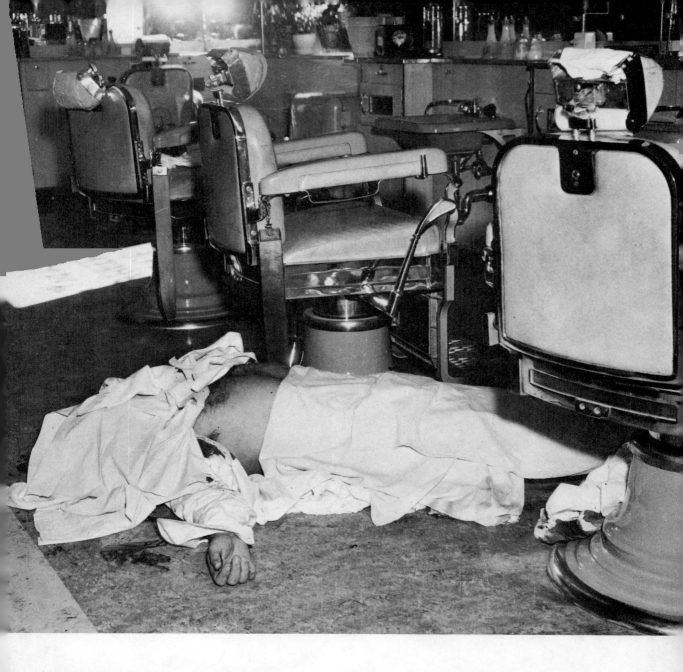

Albert Anastasia—five times
arrested for murder; one-time boss
of Murder, Inc.; former Brooklyn
waterfront hoodlum—had been in
the barber chair for 10 minutes. The
lobby door opened. Two masked men
strode in and walked directly to
chair 4, drawing guns from under
their coats. Without a word, they
pointed the guns at Anastasia's
head and began firing. Their task
done, they turned calmly and
walked out. It was a perfect gun job.

Patrons of Havana's gambling rooms
were divided about evenly between
American tourists and Cubans in
the mid-1950s.

Above, Havana's Casino Nacional. At left, Meyer Lansky, center of picture, with his wife, Teddie, leaving the Riviera Casino in Havana in February, 1958. Man in foreground is unidentified.

the coincidence weren't aware that Rothstein had been a partner with Charles A. Stoneham in a Havana casino and race track back in the twenties. Nor would they have said much about it had they known—Stoneham, after all, was remembered as a sportsman and owner of the New York Giants baseball team.

Anastasia's murder discouraged some Mafia members from attending the meeting, but the rest went ahead and gathered on schedule at the home of Joseph Barbara at Apalachin, New York. State police raided the meeting, the assembled guests fled into the bushes, and the heat went on the Mafia as never before.

The Justice Department set up a "Special Group" to probe organized crime. Among other things it picked up the trail of Nicola Gentile in Italy, and bluffed the aging and still frustrated former troubleshooter into talking freely of the old days. The Special Group recognized the need for a continuing campaign against the Syndicate, but its recommendations were ignored by the Eisenhower administration. As reaction to the Apalachin meeting died, the Special Group was disbanded. Ironically, after President John F. Kennedy became President in 1961, the basic improvements suggested by the Special Group were implemented as part of a new war on crime.

Meanwhile, a bearded Cuban named Fidel Castro proved more dangerous to Lansky's

Site of the Mafia rendezvous in Apalachin, N.Y.

Some of the convicted delegates.
Top, from left, Natal Evola,
Brooklyn, N.Y.; Anthony Riela, West
Orange, N.J. Above, John Montana,
Buffalo, N.Y.; right, Frank Majuri,
Elizabeth, N.J.

Havana empire than Anastasia and the Mafia. Everyone, including the Eisenhower administration, had managed to ignore Castro's efforts at rebellion for many months, but the Cuban people, oppressed and exploited, considered him a hero. And, as 1958 ended, the reaction to Batista and his gangster allies became more intense. The Cuban army refused to fight, and on the early morning of January 1, 1959, Batista went into exile for the second time. Lansky was right behind him. The Cuban people

first smashed parking meters and then slot machines as they waited for their new dictator to arrive and take charge of their lives.

Even as Lansky flew across the blue-green water to his home behind Gulfstream Park north of Miami, he was planning to rebuild his empire in the Bahamas. For that matter, the jet plane opened new opportunities still further away: London, Paris, Portugal, and any place else that attracted the rich and the idle.

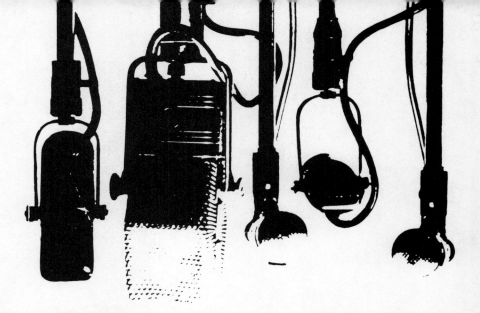

6 THE SYNDICATE INTERNATIONAL

November 8, 1960, and in the command post set up in Robert F. Kennedy's cottage in the Kennedy compound at Hyannisport, the first hard election news came in at 6:25 P.M.

It came from Campbell County, Kentucky, whose county seat was Newport and whose principal industry was illegal gambling and other forms of vice.

A few months earlier, a weary Robert Kennedy had stood in a Cincinnati hotel room and, looking out of a window at the view across the Ohio, promised a war on crime if his brother was elected.

The returns from Campbell County were considered significant since the county had managed to be on the winning side for more than one hundred years. And the first reports were optimistic—with half the returns in John Kennedy was leading Richard Nixon.

Four years earlier the Republicans had carried Campbell easily, getting 64 percent of the vote. Did the current trend perhaps indicate a massive national switch?

As the hours passed, hopes for a Kennedy sweep faded even as the Kennedy edge in Campbell County disappeared. Nixon won

in Campbell with 54.2 percent of the vote, but, nationally, Kennedy emerged the victor by a narrow margin.

The failure of the Newport-Campbell voters to be on the winning side was perhaps a forecast of bad luck to come. For within months, Robert Kennedy would be Attorney General of the United States and Newport would be the prime target of his "coordinated war on crime."

If Robert Kennedy was to be the nation's most effective Attorney General against organized crime, it was due in part at least to two unique advantages. He had personal insight into the problem as a result of his work with the Senate Permanent Investigating Subcommittee, and he had the political muscle available only to the trusted brother of the President of the United States.

As counsel to what was popularly known as the McClellan Committee, Kennedy led investigations of the International Brotherhood of Teamsters and its two corrupt leaders, Dave Beck and James R. Hoffa. Beck had been sent to prison, but Hoffa had proved a more elusive target. The long

At the McClellan Committee hearings in 1958, Chairman John L. McClellan listens while Vito Genovese, left, and his attorney, Wilfred Davis, talk. Genovese, powerful Mafia leader of the 1950s, was convicted a short time later on a conspiracy charge involving narcotics and received a 15-year prison term.

probes, however, disclosed that the union's pension funds had become a principal source of Syndicate financing. Teamster money built hotel casinos in Las Vegas, resort hotels on Miami Beach, and a lot of things in between. Hoffa was a personal friend of such men as Dalitz, and across the country his hand-picked union officials worked closely with organized crime.

Upon becoming Attorney General, Robert Kennedy set up two special units within the Justice Department—the "Get Hoffa Squad" and the Organized Crime and Anti-Racketeering Section. A spirit similar to that which had motivated the Kefauver Committee staff a decade earlier pervaded both of the new units—a youthful idealism coupled with a practical sense of power stemming from the position of the chief.

The new spirit seeped even into the sealed corridors housing the FBI, and that professional bureaucrat J. Edgar Hoover realized he was facing his most serious personal crisis since 1933. To save his job, Hoover was willing to make concessions.

Pending a showdown with Hoover, Kennedy looked for a quick victory with which to answer cynics and get his program rolling. Even as he looked, opportunity developed at Newport, Kentucky.

A citizens' revolt had been building at Newport since 1957. It was sparked, ironically enough, by a Monroe Fry article in *Esquire* which labeled Newport a "sin city" —certainly an understatement. Yet the label, and the supporting details, shocked a few good citizens of that river city. Perhaps illustrating on a national level the difficulty of mobilizing public opinion against crime was the fact that a lot of decent, hard-working, God-fearing people in Newport really didn't know how corrupt their city was. They seldom went downtown since there were no stores, no hotels, no cultural activity to compete with the facilities of Cincinnati just across the river. The casinos and bust-out joints were wide open, but a lot of church-going people had never gone inside any of them. When an occasional newspaper story mentioned gambling and prostitution, officials were quick to dismiss the charges as circulation-building sensationalism. To believe the truth, that the officials were lying to protect gangsters who paid them bribes, was more than the good citizen could do. It was easier to accept the fact that newspapers were mercenary.

Fry's article, in a national magazine, was another matter. Or so thought Christian Seifried, a middle-aged postman. He discussed the matter with his minister and won his backing to organize a "social-action committee." Other Protestant churches became interested, and a small group of dedicated "laymen" and young ministers such as George Bennett began exploring Newport. They visited the open casinos, the bust-out joints, and even penetrated into the brothels near the police stations. Satisfied that conditions were bad, but still naïve as to the reasons, the social-action committee went to Newport and Campbell County officials with hard evidence that the law was being violated. They got first a runaround, and then a brushoff. Proceeding slowly, testing and probing, the ministers waited another year before going before a Campbell grand jury. And there they learned another hard fact— the grand jury was controlled by the commonwealth's attorney, William J. Wise, who had assumed office back in the period when the Cleveland Syndicate gained control of the area. Again the brushoff.

Seifried and his little band refused to be discouraged. And when in the fall of 1958, the state's leading newspaper, the *Courier-Journal,* sent a reporter to Newport from Louisville, one hundred miles downstream, Chris sincerely considered it an answer to his prayers. The occasional hard-hitting story in the Louisville paper not only caused some heat, but forced the Cincinnati newspapers

The Justice
Department under
Robert F .Kennedy
was very effective
in harassing
organized crime.

The main street of Newport, Ky., showing the Tropicana Club, where sheriff candidate George Ratterman was framed. Below, Ratterman goes on television to tell his story. Author Hank Messick, then a newspaper reporter, is with him. Below right, crusader Christian Seifried testifying while Special Commissioner John Davis, left, looks on.

into action for competitive reasons. Slowly, through 1959 and 1960, the pressure grew in Newport. The gamblers and their allies underestimated the revolt, and by their countermoves only fanned the flames. Unhappily for them the bosses of the Cleveland Syndicate were busy in Las Vegas and Havana during the period, and Newport was left in the hands of lieutenants.

By spring in 1961 the revolt had spread to a handful of area businessmen who knew that illegal gambling and vice had stunted the town's growth. Newport's population in 1960 was a bit less than it had been in 1910. It was still the largest city in the county, but the area outside the town had more than doubled in population while Newport stood still. The more practical businessmen recognized the relation of crime to politics, and decided the only chance for reform was to elect some honest officials. The key office coming up that year was the sheriff's, and George Ratterman, ex-professional football star, attorney, and stockbroker, was persuaded to become a candidate. Once again, the gamblers and their political allies overreacted. They drugged Ratterman, took him to the Tropicana Club in Newport, and put him to bed with a stripper. Cooperative police, waiting for the call, came in and arrested the dazed Ratterman, pulled off his trousers, wrapped him in a bedsheet, and took him to the police station. But by now Newport was used to frames, and didn't believe this one. Moreover, the episode had given Kennedy's men the handle they needed—Ratterman's civil rights had been violated.

A long, dramatic struggle followed, but by November, when Ratterman was elected sheriff, the victory was won. Kennedy in his annual report to the President was able to say:

"Wagering has virtually ceased at a major gambling center, Newport, Kentucky."

The FBI, which had jurisdiction in civil rights investigations, performed well at

Newport, thus making it even more apparent that the famous agency could contribute to the war on crime if Hoover could be brought wholeheartedly into the battle. The problem was the Director's past denial that organized crime in any shape or form existed. If a way could be found to allow him to discover a new criminal organization, and get credit for the discovery, he would be off the hook.

Back under the previous administration, the Special Group had tricked Nicola Gentile into telling all he knew. His story of the early days of the Honored Society filled a thick volume, but the Special Group was disbanded before anything could be done with it. Possibly Hoover could make use of Gentile's ramblings if they could be put into the mouth of a live, believable witness. Such a witness was found in the person of Joseph Valachi, a minor New York Mafia hood who had been around in the 1930s when Maranzano and Masseria were battling. Valachi looked the part, and having killed a man in prison he was ready to make a deal. Besides, he saw a chance at vendetta—an opportunity to smear a man he hated with a fine Sicilian passion, Vito Genovese, leader of one of New York's five families.

Only one thing more was needed—a name for the new menace. Obviously it couldn't be called the Mafia since Hoover was on record as saying there was no such animal. From snatches of tape-recorded conversations, obtained by the FBI with illegal electronic "bugs," a name was found— "Cosa Nostra." It meant simply "Our Thing," and had been used by Mafia members in referring to their organization. Still, the two words might not fit easily into headlines, and that was important if the new menace was to be acceptable. The solution was to add a word. "La Cosa Nostra" might be a bit absurd for a proper name since it meant "The Our Thing," but the initials LCN could become as famous as FBI. The gimmick worked for a while, but eventually the cynical newspaper writers went back to plain old Mafia and LCN was used only by the FBI in its official reports.

Valachi was turned over to the FBI, and Gentile's manuscript was turned over to Valachi. What resulted was recorded on the televised McClellan Committee hearings, and was considered quite sensational. The FBI had done it again—and La Cosa Nostra became the new fad. Everything that conflicted with it was either twisted to fit or ignored. Kennedy aides chuckled sardonically. Hoover could call the Mafia the YWCA, they said, if by so doing he was able to let the FBI fight organized crime. These same aides had no illusions that the Mafia, or LCN, controlled crime, but they reasoned correctly that the Honored Society was small, compact, and romantic with its tales of blood oaths, omerta, and vendetta. The National Crime Syndicate, on the other hand, was too large, too diffuse, too much a part of the political and economic life of the nation to be comprehended by the average citizen. As in Newport prior to 1957, organized crime was protected by its fantastic reality. Belief required something simpler and La Cosa Nostra fit the bill. Unfortunately for the Kennedy braintrusters, however, the FBI believed its own myth, and concentrated its attention on people with Italian names. After all, everyone knew LCN was the enemy and to be a member of LCN you had to be an Italian-American. Eventually, as the FBI learned more about crime, it became necessary to invent a new classification, "associate member," to explain the roles of such men as Lansky, Dalitz, and "Sleep-out Louie" Levinson.

Had John Kennedy not been murdered, the FBI's zeal might have been controlled. But with his brother's death in 1963, Robert Kennedy was, in the words of James Hoffa, "just another lawyer," and his control over Hoover vanished. Syndicate members breathed a sigh of relief as the great

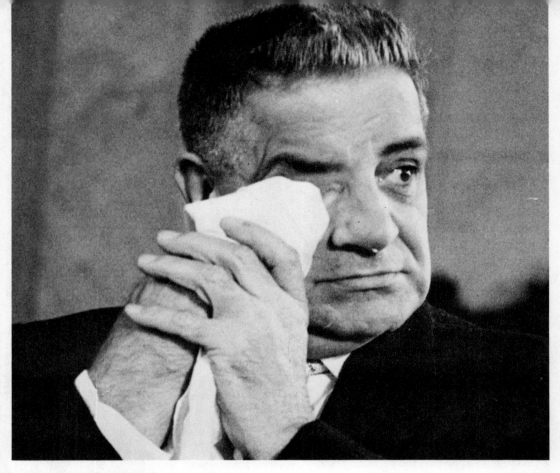

Joseph Valachi, a familiar sight to
television viewers.

coordinated war on crime degenerated into
an FBI pursuit of punks with Italian names.
As the public concentrated on Cosa Nostra,
Lansky very quietly built a new gambling
empire in the Bahamas. It was even closer
to the Gold Coast than had been the casinos
of Havana.

The fall of Newport in 1961 and subsequent pressure that closed casinos in Hot
Springs, Beaumont, Cicero, and other spots
proved among other things the wisdom of
Lansky in foreseeing the end of illegal
regional gambling centers in the United
States. The era of international activity just
beginning was but another phase of the
continuing development of organized crime.
From the point of view of Syndicate leaders,
by the time it reached full flower, conditions

in the United States would have changed in
favor of legalized gambling on a national
scale. Even as casinos opened in Freeport
and Nassau and in London and Portugal, the
drive to sell legal gambling as a painless
source of tax revenue was pushed in Miami
Beach, Atlantic City, New York, and
elsewhere.

Learning his lessons from Havana, where
a sweet setup had been lost because it
depended on the power of one man, Lansky
sought to put gambling on a broader basis in
the Bahamas. Gambling had long been illegal
in the islands, but it had also long been
tolerated for the benefit of wealthy visitors
during the winter season. Sir Stafford Sands,
a huge blob of a man who believed that you
could never have enough, was Lansky's ally

in the invasion. As leader of the Bay Street
Boys, a small group of white merchants who
ruled the black majority, Sands changed the
law to permit a "certificate of exemption" to
be issued for gambling purposes. Avowed
reason for the change was to legalize the
Bahamian Club, a posh little casino which
had operated for years, but the new law left
a loophole permitting other "certificates" to
be issued if desired. To make other members
of the Bay Street Boys desire this wouldn't
be difficult, Sands insisted, and events proved
he was right.

Another fat man, Louis Chesler, served
as front man for the casino forces. Chesler,
a Canadian promoter and friend of such
gangsters as Michael "Trigger Mike" Coppola, had helped develop several new cities
in Florida, and it was in his name that a
resort hotel, the Lucayan Beach, was built
in the piney woods of Grand Bahama Island.
One large room, listed in the plans as a
handball court, was intended for the casino.
Lansky, who approved the original plans,
later helped select the casino equipment.
Overall development of Grand Bahama was
in the hands of Wallace Groves, a former
Wall Street promoter who had served a
prison sentence for mail fraud. He was a
close friend of Sands, but was willing to cooperate with Chesler and Lansky when his
own dream of a tax-free industrial haven on
the island failed and it became necessary to
resort to tourism and gambling. In the early
days, at least, he was known as "King of
Grand Bahama" and actually had dictatorial
powers, thanks to Sir Stafford.

The grand opening of the first big casino
came on January 22, 1964, with hundreds
of jet-set "celebrities" present to give the
joint glamour. Sir Stafford Sands brought
Mrs. Ulli Lillas, a statuesque blonde of
heroic proportions who had long served as
unofficial First Lady of the Bahamas. It was
quite a bash, and no one really cared if some
of the pretty young things present were

Nassau's
world-famous
Paradise Island
Beach, popular
playground for sun
worshippers. Below,
Paradise Island
Casino, popular
playground for
gamblers.

professional call girls flown in by helicopter from Miami.

Shortly after the opening night, the truth began to leak out. The presence of professional gangsters, most of them former employees of Lansky-controlled casinos, was publicized, and hurried explanations given. Some of the more notorious names were listed as "undesirable" and told to leave as soon as capable replacements could be found. Some difficulty in finding the right people was encountered.

Chesler, whose associations with various gangsters was not easy to hide, suddenly experienced financial problems and was forced out of several companies and then off Grand Bahama entirely. Some observers suspected that Lansky was attempting to disguise his role by permitting all obvious connections to him to be cut, but how could they prove it? In this caper Lansky had perfected the part of the invisible man. When, in 1967, a royal commission of inquiry investigated Lansky's part in the development of Bahamian gambling, it noted:

"At one stage we began to wonder whether the name of Meyer Lansky was not some vast journalistic piece of fiction, so ghostly and mythical a figure did he appear."

But, as the commission decided, he was real enough.

The original program for Grand Bahama included not only the construction of a luxury hotel casino, but the sale of thousands of residential lots, the granting of business licenses, and the installation of sewer, water, electric, and telephone lines to serve the new city of Freeport. Much of this was accomplished, but the heart of the development remained the spinning roulette wheels and rolling dice in the Monte Carlo Casino.

Strangely enough, however, Groves and Chesler permitted the Mary Carter Paint Company to enter into competition with them in the development and sale of homes in Queen's Cove. Those outsiders who

This 13th-century Augustinian cloister, sitting atop a hill on Paradise Island, was shipped to the Bahamas in 2,000 pieces by Huntington Hartford.

wondered about this act of friendship didn't know that a major stockholder in Mary Carter was Thomas E. Dewey, former governor of New York and the political sponsor of Richard M. Nixon in his bid for the Vice Presidency in 1952.

Although Grand Bahama was a good site for a casino, and a second one, El Casino, was built there, the real goal of the Syndicate was Nassau, the capital of the Bahamas and long a famous resort city for the very rich. The perfect spot for a casino was on Hog Island in Nassau Harbor. All it needed was a new name, a bridge to the city, and a certificate of exemption. Huntington Hartford saw all the possibilities and all the

requirements when he bought the island several years before legal gambling came to Grand Bahama. He gave it a new name, Paradise Island, and built a small hotel, but his applications for a certificate of exemption along with his plans for a bridge were routinely denied by the Bay Street Boys. Suddenly, however, came new interest in Paradise.

On June 8, 1965, Sir Stafford Sands applied for a certificate of exemption for a casino on Paradise Island. He notified the secretary to the Cabinet that he represented the Mary Carter Paint Company and five new corporations. The certificate so avidly sought by Hartford was routinely granted

"Contact your travel agent," the ad
says, and come to beautiful
Paradise Island.

to Sands. The deal, when broken down, involved the Mary Carter Paint Company and Mrs. Wallace Groves—as an ex-convict Groves had little in his own name—with Hartford retaining a minority interest in his island. The royal commission called the arrangement "a complex of companies unnecessarily interwoven in their responsibilities, thus providing facilities for inter-company financial manoeuvres as with the complex on Grand Bahama."

One of the new companies was to build a toll bridge, from Paradise to Nassau.

Some months later, Robert Peloquin, one of the Organized Crime Section's star investigator-attorneys, probed into the complex and outlined his findings in a long memo. He concluded:

"The atmosphere seems ripe for a Lansky skim."

But the situation was in a state of flux. On October 6, 1966, the *Wall Street Journal* blew the lid off the "consultant's agreements" gambling interests had given top Bahamian officials, from the Premier on down, in return for the first certificate of exemption. The scandal, long rumored, threatened to blow the Bay Street Boys from power. Under the leadership of Lynden O. Pindling, the black majority called for new elections and for an investigation by a royal commission on inquiry. They got both. The first hearing was held on March 13, 1967, and sessions continued through the summer. But Sir Stafford Sands had an announcement: Mrs. Groves and the interests she represented were withdrawing from the Paradise Island project. Mary Carter would carry the ball alone.

Sir Stafford had very little choice. The Bay Street Boys were defeated at the polls. Pindling was the new Premier, and black power had become so real there was already talk of a break with England and independence for the crown colony.

But to achieve its goals of social progress, money was needed. If road, sewers, water,

Sir Stafford Sands, who claimed before a 1967 Commission of Inquiry that Meyer Lansky had offered him a substantial sum of money to permit gambling on Grand Bahama but that he had turned him down. At right, a recent ad.

electricity were to be provided the neglected majority, a lot of taxes would be required. And the only source of money was legal gambling—the casinos.

Anyone comparing the situation in Nassau in 1967 with what had existed in Havana in 1958 would have agreed that the glittering casinos were on much more solid ground in the Bahamas. In Cuba, the casinos depended on the private profit of a few; in the Bahamas they represented the hope of a political party and a nation. In short, the casinos in the islands rested on the same base as those in the otherwise barren state of Nevada.

Consolidation followed. Mary Carter sold its paint division and changed its name to Resorts International. And it put up $2 million to form Intertel, an agency which guaranteed to keep casinos, and other industries, free of the dread Mafia. Heading Intertel, following the assassination of Robert Kennedy in 1968, was that same Robert Peloquin who had probed the original deal on Paradise Island. Peloquin recruited a staff of former agents and opened branch offices around the country and in Canada.

The sales pitch of Intertel was the promise that legal casino gambling could be kept clean. When Resorts International, which was very interested in expanding, took an option on property in New Jersey, it sent spokesmen to advocate legal gambling before a legislative committee. Intertel was also represented, assuring the legislators that the Mafia could be screened out of any casino operated by Resorts International. Despite the assurances, the bill to legalize was voted down, but everyone knew the issue would return.

Intertel's biggest coup came, however, when the mysterious Howard Hughes allegedly turned over to the agency security operations at his Las Vegas casinos and allowed Intertel to fly him to Paradise Island and guard his cherished privacy. Possibly Hughes figured that if Lansky could be invisible in the Bahamas, it would be easy for him to do the same.

Hughes had moved into Las Vegas in 1967, buying the Desert Inn from the Cleveland Syndicate, and expanding to become the largest casino owner in Nevada. His arrival was hailed as the beginning of a new era free of Mob influence. Three years later the same words were used when he departed—under Intertel the Mob would really be rooted out. The Las Vegas *Sun,* not the most objective journalistic voice, suggested that Intertel was the Mob's private police agency, but Peloquin and his aides continued to issue claims that would have sold Ivory Soap.

The propaganda was made plausible by one basic fact—the men who began as bootleggers were getting old and tired. Power was passing to a younger generation. The new leaders had college training and no criminal records. Twenty years might pass before a new Gentile came along to put words into the mouth of a new Valachi and shock the American people with new tales of Syndicate activity. Thus in 1971 it was easy for Intertel, and the FBI, to claim a crushing victory in the battle against the Mafia. A lot of old capos had been jailed, but few people noted that they represented at the height of their power only a fraction of the syndicate's strength. Newspapers across the country took their cue from the

When billionaire Howard Hughes
and other industrialists began to
move into Las Vegas in the late
1960s and take over the casinos,
it was hoped that the Mob's control
over gambling would be lessened.
Below, gambling at the Dunes
Hotel in 1967.

metropolitan press of New York, where for years the coverage of crime was largely limited to "climbing" the Mafia family tree and guessing which capo was now the boss of all the bosses. New Yorkers, by and large, remained as ignorant of conditions in the 1970s as they were in the days of the Masseria-Maranzano war. Years before, men like Lansky and his close friend Vincent "Jimmy Blue Eyes" Alo, learned that once out of New York they would be ignored, while comparatively minor punks with Italian names got the headlines. Every ten or fifteen years a "blue-ribbon commission" would be formed in New York to discover all over again that the police department was corrupt, that gambling and prostitution were rife,

that bribery was a way of life. That these conditions were so obvious a cub reporter could have found them, had a cub reporter been so assigned, apparently never occurred to anyone. And crime and corruption continued to flourish.

Much of the apparent progress in combating the Mafia was due to the "strike-force" concept begun under Attorney General Ramsey Clark. It was a variation of the "coordinated war" begun by Robert Kennedy, differing only in that strike-force chiefs were assigned to a given area on a semi-permanent basis instead of in a hit-and-run, specific case program.

Ironically, Clark became a campaign issue in the 1968 election, with Candidate Nixon

At right, Vincent "Jimmy Blue Eyes" Alo, Meyer Lansky's closest Mafia associate. Far right, Joseph Colombo, Sr., who tried hard to be known as a new kind of Mafia boss, is shot, allegedly by Mafia rivals, at an Italian-American Unity Day ceremony in June, 1971.

Attorney General Ramsey Clark discusses federal anticrime coordination. Clockwise starting at upper right: Deputy Atty. General Warren Christopher; OEO director Sargent Shriver; HUD Secy. Robert C. Weaver; Clark; Labor Secy. Willard Wirtz; HEW Undersecy. Wilbur Cohen; Asst. Atty. General (Criminal Division) Fred Vinson.

promising to replace him if elected with a "real" crime-fighter. John Mitchell did succeed him, but Mitchell's chief contribution was to expand the number of strike forces and to force J. Edgar Hoover to allow the FBI to give at least token cooperation.

It was Mitchell who bowed to political pressure from newly organized Italian-Americans and ordered the FBI to quit using the terms "Mafia," "La Cosa Nostra," or even "LCN." The campaign by the Italian-Americans was patterned after the fight long waged by the Anti-Defamation League of B'nai B'rith. Gangsters such as Lansky had hidden behind the ADL for years, screaming loudly that their critics were anti-Semitic at heart. Belatedly some of the Mafia boys got wise and tried the same trick. Joe Colombo, by making the FBI retreat, attracted so much prestige it became inevitable that one of his rivals would try to have him knocked off. Call it what you please, the Honored Society was still a jealous, vendetta-ridden brotherhood.

Yet, no thanks to the FBI, the Mafia was dying off. It had been dying since the Bugs and Meyer Mob knocked off Maranzano for Lucky Luciano. As third- and fourth-generation Americans came along, as they moved out of the ghettos; as they, in short, became Americanized, there was no longer a need or an excuse for the Mafia. The conditions that had spawned it in Sicily and permitted it to take root in America no longer existed.

Best evidence of its decline in the 1960s came in the Miami area where a new minority group began seeking the easy way to wealth and power. Federal officials named them the "Cuban Mafia."

It began in Havana when Lansky put Batista back in power and built his gambling empire there. He made league with Cuban gangsters, training them, educating them, corrupting them if they were not already

In the January, 1972, Miami heroin seizure, two Cubans, five Puerto Ricans, and an Argentinian were arrested. At right, federal narcotics agents in a private home where they found 178 pounds of heroin in suitcases.

corrupt enough. When Batista fled from Castro, the native gangsters also sought new homes. Those with money in Swiss banks went to Spain or South America. Those without came to Miami. In the years that followed thousands of honest Cubans fled communism, and the gangsters among them were quick to pose as patriots. When many real patriots died in 1961 at the Bay of Pigs in that ill-fated attempt to invade Cuba, the gangsters were waiting in Nassau and other Caribbean ports to follow the troops into Havana and reopen the casinos.

As hopes faded for a return to power in Cuba, the exiles looked around for another source of quick wealth. They found it in the cocaine traffic. Unlike other narcotics, there is little legitimate use for cocaine, so facilities for manufacturing it were few. The drug is obtained from the coca leaf grown in the Andes Mountains of South America. It was thus far out of normal channels of Mafia activity.

The Cubans around the world pooled their resources, and contacted old Syndicate friends they had known in Havana. Cocaine began to appear in Miami in greater and greater amounts. Moreover, as the price of heroin soared when the supply failed to keep pace with the demand, the cost of cocaine remained stable. In a few years it was selling for half the price of heroin, and it was becoming more and more popular.

Federal narcotics agents held their breath, expecting a gang war to develop when what they now called the "Italian Mafia" discovered the competition was costing it money. But nothing happened. It was soon revealed that old-line Mafia gangsters

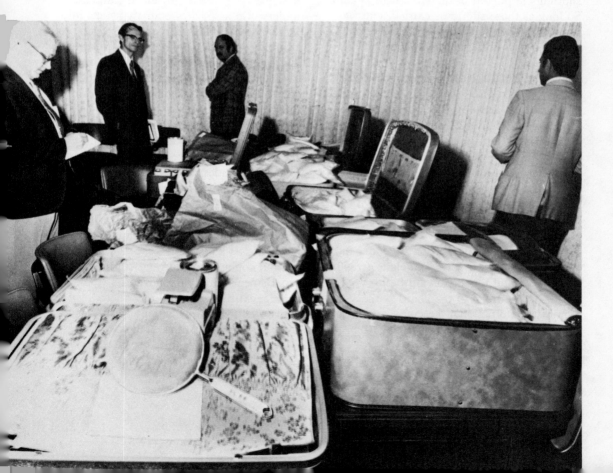

were cooperating with the upstart Cubans. Not only were they permitting them to sell cocaine, they were turning over much of the heroin traffic to them as well.

Investigation uncovered the shadowy outlines of an international organization operating in Europe, South America, and the United States. But much time would pass before newspapers could begin playing games with the "Cuban Mafia" family tree, for only a handful of middle-management executives had been identified by 1971. Agents guessed that an "International Mr. Big" and a "Domestic Mr. Big" existed, but they didn't really know.

Moreover, even as the reality of the new organized group was acknowledged, observers saw crowding on its heels what they began calling the "Puerto Rican Mafia." And after that, the "Black Mafia," unless social conditions changed to the point where minority groups had no need to seek shortcuts in pursuit of the American Dream. So long as those shortcuts existed, and were profitable, so long would organized crime remain a part of the socio-economic life of the nation.

As if to illustrate the time of transition, Meyer Lansky in 1970 left his adopted homeland for Israel. Lansky, who had survived King Solomon, Dutch Schultz, Lepke, Bugsy Siegel, Joe Adonis, Longie Zwillman, Lucky Luciano, Albert Anastasia, Vito Genovese, and scores of others, knew he was scheduled to be indicted for skimming funds from the Flamingo. He arrived in Israel many months in advance of the indictment, however, and was greeted as a "socialite" and "philanthropist." Under the "Law of the Return" he could claim Israeli citizenship, and this he obviously intended to do. As chairman of the board of the Syndicate International, he could operate just as easily—perhaps more easily—from Tel Aviv as Miami Beach.

The publication of a biography, *Lansky,* in the United States in April, 1971, caused a crisis for Meyer. The Israeli newspaper *Ha'aretz* serialized the book and demanded that Lansky be expelled. Moreover, stung by the book's suggestion that Lansky was given advance warning to get out of the country, the Justice Department rushed through an immediate indictment. Later, the indictment was superseded by a stronger one as the probe of the Flamingo in Las Vegas was completed.

With the spotlight on Israel, it soon became obvious that the embattled little country had become a sanctuary for gangsters of Jewish descent. Scores of them were there—from Joseph "Doc" Stacher to Phil "the Stick" Kovolick. Lansky became the symbol of a broader issue. *Newsweek* summed up the question in a November 29, 1971, article:

"To many critics in the press, however, the government's stand appeared to be motivated by self-interest. Each year, these newspapers pointed out, Lansky and his underworld associates pour vast sums into Israeli bonds and Israeli philanthropies. As the daily *Ha'aretz* saw it, the government seemed afraid of losing the millions of dollars in illicit money first 'laundered' in mob-controlled institutions and then funneled into Israeli business and industry."

Whatever the outcome of Lansky's personal struggle, the affair had again bared the sophisticated nature of organized crime. Over the decades millions upon millions had been placed in Swiss banks and invested around the world. Gangsters had influenced foreign policy, financed revolutions, elected senators, governors, and perhaps Presidents. Their bosses had become captains of industry and commerce, and were considered "sportsmen" and "philanthropists." The average citizen could not tell where legal activity ended and illegal enterprise began. In reality, he didn't want to know.

And that, perhaps, was organized crime's greatest achievement.

A PARTIAL CHRONOLOGY

A PARTIAL CHRONOLOGY OF EVENTS IMPORTANT TO THE DEVELOPMENT OF ORGANIZED CRIME IN THE UNITED STATES

1898 Arnold Rothstein becomes a high-school dropout in New York City.

1900 Immigrants continue to arrive in great numbers.

1902 Big Jim Colosimo marries a Chicago madam and organizes a white-slave ring.

1903 Nicola Gentile arrives illegally from Sicily and becomes a Mafia troubleshooter.

1908 The Bureau of Investigation, later famous as the FBI, is formed.

1910 Mann Act intended to end white slavery becomes law and sets precedent for federal police action in matters involving interstate commerce.

1912 Owney "the Killer" Madden becomes boss of the Gophers in New York.

1913 Arthur "Mickey" McBride becomes newspaper "circulator" in Cleveland as newspaper wars provide training for future gangsters.

1917 United States enters World War I and J. Edgar Hoover becomes a clerk in the Justice Department.

1919 Gamblers advised by Arnold Rothstein "fix" the World Series.

1920 Volstead Act to enforce constitutional ban on liquor becomes effective . . . John "the Fox" Torrio takes charge of murdered Colosimo's empire in Chicago . . . Rothstein experiments with rumrunning in New York . . . Warren Harding elected President as voters seek "normalcy."

1921 "Ohio Gang" goes to Washington with Harding and era of corruption begins . . . George Remus becomes "King of the Bootleggers" as first phase of Prohibition begins.

1923 President Harding dies suddenly but pursuit of the fast buck continues as public and private policy.

1924 J. Edgar Hoover promoted to boss of Bureau of Investigation . . . Al Capone conquers Cicero, Illinois, when Torrio's peaceful penetration fails . . . Bugs and Meyer Mob operates in New York under leadership of Meyer Lansky.

1925 Al Capone takes charge in Chicago as Torrio quits in disgust . . . Pioneer rumrunner "Big Bill" Dwyer convicted in New York, but Frank Costello goes free.

1926 Moe Dalitz quits Detroit Purple Gang to join with Morris Kleinman, Samuel Tucker, and Louis Rothkopf to form the Cleveland Syndicate.

1928 Mafia civil war results in abortive "Grand Council" meeting in Cleveland.

1929 St. Valentine Day Massacre fails in its purpose but gives Chicago something to brag about . . . Torrio helps create alliance of bootleggers known as "Big Seven" at Atlantic City meeting . . . Stock Market crash on October 29 marks beginning of economic depression which gives organized crime its big chance to get roots down.

1931 Joe "the Boss" Masseria murdered by Lucky Luciano on April 15 as Mafia civil war ends . . . Salvatore Maranzano murdered by the Bugs and Meyer Mob on behalf of the "Combination" on September 11 as Mafia is "Americanized" and given a secondary role in crime . . . Capone convicted.

1932 Franklin D. Roosevelt's election is defeat of big-city political bosses.

1933 Banks close, forcing businessmen to turn to gangsters . . . Molaska, Inc., formed on November 25, a few days before Prohibition ends. Torrio forms Prendergast-Davies to sell liquor legally.

1934 National Crime Syndicate formed along NRA lines and "Murder, Inc.," created as enforcement arm.

1935 Thomas E. Dewey appointed special prosecutor in New York . . . Dutch Schultz, last of the independents, murdered by the National Crime Syndicate.

1936 Dewey sends Charles "Lucky" Luciano to prison, but Lansky promises to get him out.

1937 "Big Heat" begins as Louis "Lepke" Buchalter becomes most wanted man and The Mob discovers America. Lansky goes to Cuba and Benjamin "Bugsy" Siegel goes to California.

1939 Torrio, like Capone, convicted on tax charges . . . Lepke surrenders, ending Big Heat . . . Germany invades Poland, closing Havana gambling joints . . . Sir Stafford Sands creates legal machinery to permit gambling in the Bahamas . . . Moses Annenberg, father of the bookie wire service, pleads guilty to tax evasion and turns his empire over to Mickey McBride who reorganizes it as Continental Press.

1940 Cleveland Syndicate expands into Kentucky at Newport . . . Abe Reles sings about Murder, Inc., fingers Lepke, Siegel, others..

1941 Lepke is sentenced to die . . . Reles, under guard, is murdered and Siegel beats the rap.

1942 Thomas E. Dewey becomes governor of New York.

1943 Leaders of the Chicago Syndicate are indicted on March 18 in movie-extortion plot. Nitti kills himself the same day, but others eventually win quick parole . . . Operation Underworld features Lansky and Luciano helping Naval Intelligence win the war and making Lansky acting boss of the Mafia.

1944 Gangsters get rich in black market activity and prepare for postwar expansion . . . Batista flees Cuba after free election and comes to Florida.

1945 Casino era begins as Lansky operates in Florida, New York, Louisiana, Nevada, New Jersey, and elsewhere.

1947 Bugsy Siegel opens his dream casino, the Flamingo, and then is murdered on June 20. Nevada gambling boom begins.

1948 Fuller Warren elected governor of Florida in prologue to attempt by Chicago Syndicate to muscle in on S & G Syndicate in Miami Beach . . . Cleveland Syndicate invests in Desert Inn on Las Vegas "Strip."

1950 Kefauver Committee begins hearings, Florida casinos closed.

1951 Kefauver Committee puts finger on Frank Costello in pioneer television spectacular in New York. Goes out of business after exposing links between crime, business, and politics . . . Senator Joseph McCarthy sees Red.

1952 McCarthy hysteria diverts public interest from real gangsters to alleged Reds . . . The country likes Ike and elects Dwight D. Eisenhower President . . . Batista regains power in Cuba with help from Lansky.

1953 Lansky spends three months in prison in New York, then moves to Hollywood, Florida . . . Joe Adonis ordered deported.

1954 Lansky begins building new gambling empire in Cuba.

1955 Hawksbill Creek Act makes ex-convict Wallace Groves the "King of Grand Bahama" Island.

1957 Frank Costello wounded and deposed . . . Albert Anastasia challenges Lansky in Cuba and is murdered . . . Mafia meeting at Apalachin, N.Y., is a fiasco . . . "Special Group" created in Justice Department to fight organized crime . . . James R. Hoffa replaces David Beck as boss of the Teamsters Union and its pension funds.

1959 Batista and Lansky flee Cuba as Fidel Castro takes over and closes casinos . . . Abner "Longie" Zwillman dies mysteriously.

1960 "Special Group" in Justice Department is disbanded . . . John F. Kennedy defeats Vice-President Richard M. Nixon . . . Lansky shows his hand in the Bahamas.

1961 Robert F. Kennedy becomes Attorney General and begins a "coordinated" war on crime . . . FBI begins mass bugging of Mafia telephones . . . George Ratterman survives frame to close down Newport . . . Bay of Pigs disaster ends Mafia hopes for Cuban gambling revival.

1962 "Trigger Mike" Coppola, boss of numbers racket in Harlem, pleads guilty to tax charges in Miami after his wife tells all to IRS agents Richard Jaffe and Joseph Wanderschied.

1963 Joseph Valachi sings Nicola Gentile's old, sad song and the FBI "discovers" La Cosa Nostra . . . President Kennedy is murdered in Dallas.

1964 First gambling casino opens on Grand Bahama Island with Lansky's men in control . . . Crime war falters as FBI concentrates on gangsters with Italian names.

1967 Bay Street Boys defeated in Bahama election but gambling remains essential industry . . . James R. Hoffa goes to prison . . . Howard Hughes buys Desert Inn and other Las Vegas casinos but remains invisible.

1968 Paradise Island Casino opens in Nassau with Richard M. Nixon as guest of honor and Thomas E. Dewey a secret stockholder . . . Robert F. Kennedy assassinated while campaigning for presidential nomination . . . Nixon elected President.

1969 John Mitchell becomes Attorney General . . . Mary Carter Paint Company becomes Resorts International . . . "Cuban Mafia" begins peaceful take-over of narcotics traffic.

1970 Drive to establish legal gambling casinos defeated in Miami Beach . . . Lansky escapes to Israel well in advance of indictment and declares plans to become Israeli citizen.

1971 Joe Colombo, latest Mafia leader, seriously wounded in New York . . . Joe Adonis dies in exile . . . President Nixon commutes Hoffa's sentence and sends him home for Christmas.

PICTURE CREDITS

Burt Goldblatt wishes to thank the following people for their help in getting picture material for this book: John Bond, Lew Morris and Jo Ann Pellegrino, National Park Service; Truman R. Strowbridge, United States Coast Guard historian; Mark Ethridge, editor, and Janet E. Cashin, assistant librarian, Detroit *Free Press;* Dr. Harvey L. Benovitz; Dr. Morris Hymann; Ptl. David Bronstein, New York City Police Museum; Det. Frank Giugliano and Ptl. Eugene Fitzpatrick, New York City Police Department; James Smith, Microfilm Department, Columbia University Library; Monte Arnold, Lincoln Center Theater Collection; the staff of the New York Public Library; Russell Lynes; Stuart Harris; Sally Williams; and Cynthia Vartan.

United Press International

10 L, 16 B, 23, 26 R, 27 R, 28 TR, 38 T, 49, 52, 55, 60, 64 L, 66, 68 T, 73, 74, 75 B, 76, 78, 88, 89 T, 92 T, 93 T&B, 94 T, 97, 98 T, 98 B, 99 TL, 99 TR, 103 R, 104 T&B, 105 T&B, 107, 132, 133, 134, 135, 139, 141, 147 L&R, 150 T, 158, 160, 163, 164, 167, 168, 171, 178, 179, 183, 185, 189, 194, 196, 197, 199, 201

Brown Brothers

13, 16 T, 24 R, 33, 35, 36, 41 R, 45, 69, 70, 79 T, 82, 85 B, 89 B, 92 B, 116, 120, 126, 142, 145, 174, 175

Authors' collection

4, 11, 22 T, 24 L, 32 T, 40 (all), 41 T&B, 42, 44 L, 50, 61, 64 R, 65 T&B, 68 B, 71, 77 T&B, 81 T&B, 90 R, 94 B, 99 TR, 103 T&B, 103 T&B, 122, 123, 124, 137, 150 B, 151, 152, 153, 154, 155, 156, 157, 177, 186, 187, 198

Detroit *Free Press*

57 T, 79 B, 85 T, 95, 100, 101, 118

New York Public Library

12 B, 31, 37, 38 B, 44 R, 56 T, 57 B, 115

Lincoln Center Theater Collection

26 T&B, 75 T

Chicago Historical Society

20, 62 T&B, 162

New York *Daily News*

24 T, 25 B

National Archives

86, 87

Wide World

2, 3, 27 L, 28 TL, 59, 91, 102 T, 129, 136, 140, 147 B, 159 C, 165, 172, 176, 187 T, 202, 203

National Park Service

14, 29 T&B

Columbia University Library

12 T, 17 L, 18 B, 25 T, 32 B, 39, 45 T, 47 B, 51 B, 53, 54, 63 R, 74 T, 109, 114, 118 T, 148, 159 T&B, 166, 174 T, 180

Bahama Tourist News Bureau

191 T&B, 192, 193, 195

INDEX

212